CRIME INVESTIGATED

JACK THE RIPPER

CATCH ME WHEN YOU CAN

igloobooks

Published in 2014
by Igloo Books Ltd
Cottage Farm
Sywell
NN6 0BJ
www.igloobooks.com

Project managed by HL Studios

HUN001 0214
2 4 6 8 10 9 7 5 3 1
ISBN 978-1-78197-961-7

Printed and manufactured in China

Contents

Introduction

The Ripper of Victorian London

The Ripper of Victorian London

To modern eyes, the dark age of Jack the Ripper in the London of 1888 is the stuff of countless nightmares. For those who lived there at the time, every waking moment was a hellish reality.

The Ripper may have been a 'savage' at heart, but he embraced the latest learning and technology of the Victorian era. An examination of his victims revealed that he had certain surgical knowledge. Their mutilation was of a special kind. Contemporary reports suggested that Jack was well-dressed, educated and perhaps even high born: a man of society, a gentleman in every respect. Yet that is all. The identity of this depraved killer, who so gruesomely cut into his victims, may never be known and this has provoked endless fascination and speculation over the years. It is acknowledged that there are five victims that definitely can be attributed to Jack the Ripper, although there are thirteen other unsolved murders in this area of London, which showed similar modus operandi. This would take the tally of Ripper victims to 18 making him one of the first members of that particular breed of criminal, the serial killer.

Victorian London

In order to understand the territory where the Ripper prowled, one needs to understand the ambience and society of Victorian London. The London of that time was not just the colourful, hectic city portrayed through period dramas or the Sherlock Holmes stories. There was sharp division between the social classes. In one part of the city flourished a gritty, seedy, violent part of society that was a world removed from the prosperous lifestyle of the upper-class world a few miles away. The Ripper murders occurred in an area of the capital that in the 1880s was highly impoverished. The poverty of Victorian London is unimaginable to many today. Conditions were squalid and lethal. People starved and died.

One of the most impoverished areas was the East End, in what is now known as the London Borough of Tower Hamlets. Within Tower Hamlets is the area of Whitechapel, which was the killing ground where the murders of the five women – the so-termed Five Canonical victims – took place. This is why some of the primary sources of the time call Jack not 'The Ripper', but also 'The Whitechapel Murderer' and 'The Leather Apron'.

Chapter 1

A Murderer in Victorian London

A Murderer in Victorian London

Victorian London is often sensationalised in television and literature, with writers' using creative license to conjure up fantastical tales of monsters and legends. The Victorian Period that we read and watch in these creations of fiction are steeped in fog, with the sound of carriage wheels clattering across cobblestones. A sense of terror on the streets. We watch from the comfort of our modern lives, however, for the inhabitants of Victorian London, the horror was very real and on their doorstep.

Jack the Ripper's reign of terror occurred during the two years of 1888 and 1889. Writers constantly revisit the murders that today still baffle and enthral, but no single image of Jack has been determined. Descriptions range from the possible to the far-fetched: He was a surgeon who had lost his mind, or a vampire who rose from the dead each night. People have turned to psychic forces and criminal profiling to solve the crimes and there is even a group dedicated to the search – Ripperologists.

Everything from death certificates through to inquest reports has been carefully evaluated for clues and there are specific publications, groups, and online forums that allow investigators to share any research that comes to light.

Indeed, everyone has their pet theory on the identity of Jack the Ripper and which of the many Whitechapel murders over the two years were actually down to him. The only certainty is that during 1888 and 1889, many women were murdered, most of them were prostitutes, and at least five were taken by a killer, who used the same modus operandi with increasing violence. He had access to a sharp blade some 15.2cm to 20.3cm long. Finally, the type of damage to his victims demonstrated that the killer must have had some experience or education regarding the human body, particularly the organs. Many researchers believe that Jack worked in the medical profession, or was a butcher with rudimentary knowledge of anatomy. Over the years, the number of suspects has grown. But the truth remains elusive. In some cases, forgeries have occurred, or evidence has been invented.

A Time of Progress

The period 1837–1901, when Queen Victoria ruled, saw a period of massive change and evolution as the effects of industrialisation filtered through society. By the 1880s, people in the growing middle class were prospering, but at the lower end of the social scale good money was scarce. Here another trade flourished: Prostitution. It was easy but dangerous. It cost many women their lives. At this time, campaigners began to speak out against prostitution targeting it as 'The Great Social Evil'. They said it undermined goals to reduce poverty, with the slums a personal affront to women and progress. The movement against prostitution was bolstered by the Contagious Diseases Act of 1864, which permitted constables to forcibly inspect any woman suspected of having venereal disease. Reforms were made to instil morality into the slums by closing down brothels.

Writers portrayed prostitutes as victims of poverty, or fallen women who had become corrupted. Assumptions were made about why the women did what they did, but the truth was that no one truly looked into the reasons behind their behaviour. Divorce had changed. The Matrimonial Causes Act of 1857 permitted men, but not women, to divorce over adultery. Putting a woman 'out on to the street' was made far easier than it had been in the past. However, it was the sheer numbers of people in London that encouraged, and increased, the number of prostitutes on the street, and made closing down the practice so difficult. Many women found it difficult to raise enough money to live and so looked for additional work. The desperate turned to drink, and alcoholism became a problem. These changes were unique in history. Over the course of the 1800s, many of the homes and buildings in London and the bigger cities would be transformed forever. Properties were changed into smaller homes for rent with the tenants living virtually on top of one another. In some situations, there were as many as thirty people living in a single room.

Yet though the area was teeming with people the quietness surrounding the Ripper murders was eerie. While neighbours could not have conversations without being overheard, these murders were committed seemingly without witnesses. No one was aware anything untoward had occurred until the woman's body was discovered. Afterwards, suspects were not hard to find, although hard evidence was. It was not uncommon for sailors and soldiers to be out drinking for the night. In at least one eyewitness report, men seen earlier with the victim were believed to be sailors. Yet the ability for easy travel by horse carriage or the newly introduced railways made many possibilities available to a killer who could vanish before anyone was alerted. None of the crime scenes included footprints or any sign of someone leaving the location. The police thought it likely the criminal lived in or near to Whitechapel.

During this time, records were difficult to obtain, particularly for women who lived rough. However, the women killed in Whitechapel had dealings with workhouses, which kept details, so enabling at least some of their past to be tracked. Many of the Ripper victims did not stay at any particular workhouse for long and were only given a bed for a night or two. Homeless individuals were considered inferior to the 'deserving poor'. More than one of the victims of the Ripper had been out for the night plying their trade to get money for a place to sleep. The poor were often dirty and many were sick, often with curable conditions that had simply worsened from lack of care. Infirmaries were open around London and Whitechapel, but not all women took care of all illnesses. Most prostitutes of the time were described as filthy and missing teeth, and diseases were not uncommon. Women living from room to room did not generally enjoy the benefits of clean clothing or regular bathing and the state of some of the Whitechapel murder victims drew unfavourable comment.

Prostitutes of the time were so poor, that in very few of the murders was theft even considered a possible motive for the crime. In many cases, it was strongly suggested that Jack the Ripper was in fact a 'Jill, scorned by men and filled with hatred and anger as she sought out women. She might have been a resentful wife, or a woman who lost her man to venereal disease caught from prostitutes. One of the many strange aspects of the Ripper murders is the age of the victims. Although one of the Canonical Five was said to have been in her mid-20s, most of the Whitechapel murder victims were women in their late 30s or early 40s. At that time it was more likely that girls under 18 would be walking the streets and while young prostitutes were far less likely to be working the slums, they were probably more numerous than older females. A few of the Whitechapel victims, women had left homes with husbands and children. Some may have suffered from mental illness.

The killing spree kept many people off the streets and behind locked doors. Even the prostitutes sought escorts after dark. The exact tally of Ripper victims may never be known. Some crimes could not be investigated as crimes because, incredibly, they were reported as accidents. Perhaps to enhance their own reputation and to prevent any social panic, law enforcers in the 1800s were anxious to maintain that public order was being kept. To keep this up, some crimes were downgraded when filed. Thus stolen property was recorded as lost, and a violent death became suicide. During this time, unclaimed bodies ran the risk of such classification, particularly where it could easily be claimed the body showed signs of suffocation rather than strangulation. This particular problem prevents researchers from knowing for certain that all the Ripper victims have been identified. There are theories that the Ripper may have had victims prior to his acknowledged kills. It is something that perhaps we will never find out.

Meanwhile, another audience discovered the dark streets of Whitechapel and liked them. The newspapers of the day realised that their readers enjoyed sensationalism and were fascinated by the unfolding drama. One headline read, 'Ghastly Murder in the East End.'

Reporters searched everywhere for clues and information regarding the killer. They hoped to uncover the truth before the police, and when this could not be done they had their own answers and suppositions. In some cases, they falsified evidence to liven up the tale.

Newspapers printed letters supposedly from the Ripper himself, as well as ones they had written themselves. Journalists evaluated every person brought in for questioning. In one instance, a newspaper was even sued by a suspect, who won his case when the police released him. Each murder brought fresh fear to the readers, and reporters tried to fill in the gaps for readers. Numerous letters were received by both police and newspapers, claiming responsibility for the mutilations, or tipping off who they believed to be behind them. It was from one of these letters that the name 'Jack the Ripper' was first introduced. The 'Dear Boss Letter', was one of many letters that became famous pieces of evidence, though no one has ever been certain that they were actually written by the culprit. In some cases, the letters are clearly written by different individuals. Much of what was published in the newspapers highlighted the case but the police were still unable to close the matter. It was claimed that they were badly equipped and incompetent even though there was then little evidence that could have resulted in an arrest.

The last of the Canonical Five killings came in November 1888 although the terror continued; however, no one had any idea that the killings were over; they were simply waiting for the next victim. In some cases, women would take advantage of this fear by threatening to scream when men refused to do as they asked; in other cases it was believed that a butcher was causing general panic. On one occasion a police chase became a mob hunt for a man, who turned out to be innocent. It was dangerous during this time to threaten a woman in public for fear of mob response. It is believed that at least one woman took advantage of the publicity to rob a person she had brought back to her home.

The likely truth is that Jack the Ripper successfully eluded capture because of careful planning. For a criminal, the Victorian period provided great cover: Transport included trains to take you swiftly far away from the crime scene and slums to trawl for anonymous victims. There was, of course, no access to the technology utilised today by police with genetic analysis, fingerprinting, or profiling. The police claimed they did their best, although the newspapers were critical. Constables patiently walked their beat in an attempt to keep women safe; however, none of these measures seemed to be enough. On more than one occasion, reports demonstrated that the constable had actually been close to a murder, but was in the wrong area at the wrong time. In any event, it was a challenge to have enough police positioned around the key danger spots, and even tougher to try to question anyone who might have seen or heard anything after each death. Many local police voiced their theories over whom the suspect might be; however, none was as influential in the research, which has survived through today, as Sir Melville Macnaghten of Scotland Yard. We shall hear from him later.

Chapter 2

Women's Work
in Whitechapel

Women's Work
in Whitechapel

Many factory owners preferred female workers over males, as they were more willing to work harder and without complaint because they often had children to support. It was common for pregnant women to work till they were in labour and return as soon as possible after the birth. A law passed in 1891 that allowed women to take a break from factory work for at least four weeks after having a baby. However, despite its good intentions, the law was ignored by many women as they were unable to afford the time off without any pay.

During the Victorian era, London was the hub of commerce, culture, transport and communication. Yet despite its affluence, the city also had an ugly side particularly with slum areas such as Whitechapel in the East End. Housing and employment was desperate and crime was rife. Urban development in other parts of London led to an influx of displaced people, making the situation worse. Life in Whitechapel was squalid and while it affected everyone, women suffered more, both with their work and family.

No one knows why Jack the Ripper chose this area to commit his appalling crimes, but perhaps its downtrodden state made things easier for him.

Living Conditions

The Industrial Revolution in Britain changed everything. It disrupted the social order, made fortunes for the lucky few and misery for many. Slums developed as the population grew and people flooded into the cities in search of work. During the 17th century, the Whitechapel district was relatively prosperous, but as London went through rapid urbanisation during the mid 18th century, the district had to deal with overcrowding that led to a massive demand for cheap housing.

By the second half of the 19th century, the area had the city's worst slums. One year, 4,000 houses in the district were deemed as uninhabitable with the inhabitants suffering from malnutrition and disease. Children had a 50 per cent chance of living beyond five years of age. People lived day in and day out in unbearable filth and stench. House cellars were often filled with liquid sewage as there was no sanitation system, the air was foul from factory fumes and chimney smoke.

For many families, home was a crowded, single-room accommodation without sanitation or proper ventilation. The district also had more than 200 common lodging houses that served as a shelter for the homeless and the destitute. The lodging houses, also known as doss houses, would allow 80 or so people to cramp into a tiny dormitory. In the old currency of four pennies, one could sleep on a bed little different from a coffin placed on the ground. Two pennies would allow an individual to lean against a rope that had been tied along the length of the room. Every night, these houses would take in a total of about 8,000 individuals – men, women, and children. Living conditions were harsh and people had to adapt to survive.

Children were not spared the harsh conditions. It was common for them to start working at an early age to provide food for their families. Whitechapel gradually became transformed from a market area into an impoverished district where the conditions and deprived lifestyles would come together to create a toxic violent environment.

Occupations and Class

The early part of the 19th century saw the growth of the middle and working classes, but with the upper class retaining political control. This led to tensions and hostility. There was a huge gap between the different sections in the working class. For instance, the income and living conditions for a skilled labourer were much better than those of an unskilled labourer.

At the bottom of the class system was what was described as the 'underclass' or the 'sunken people' – a section of society well below the poverty line made up of the unemployed, as well as the sick and injured.

By the time Whitechapel was transformed into an urban housing area to support the influx of immigrants, many of London's manufacturing processes had moved to the northern part of the United Kingdom to take advantage of cheaper raw materials, land and labour. In the metropolitan areas of the city, a growing number of people found work as clerks, dockers, painters, decorators and upholsterers. Whitechapel became popular with Irish, Russian and Jewish immigrants. In fact, the Jewish population rose to more than 50,000 within just ten years. However, the rise in population was not matched by a rise in working opportunities. It was during this time that the boundaries between the different classes became more marked than ever. The inhabitants of the Whitechapel district could be classified into three sub-classes:

- Poor – The poor class comprised of individuals who had a meagre, yet fairly stable source of income. They included shopkeepers and tailors, as well as men in construction and manufacturing, such as labourers, builders and dockworkers.

- Very poor – While the income of poor people in the district was already very low, women and children suffered more. Owing to the high mortality rate of men, their widows were left to raise children on their own. They took up odd jobs that paid minimum wages, working as seamstresses, clothes washers, or weavers.

- Homeless – The Whitechapel district saw plenty of people who were practically homeless. They lived in a permanent state of deprivation and rarely found employment.

Life in Whitechapel was a struggle for everyone. This struggle had a terrible spin-off. The lack of stability in the social and economic lives of the population made it even more difficult for officials to catch the Ripper. Men could find occasional work with odd jobs down by the docks. But without any employment or accommodation records, only a few of the inhabitants in the district left a trace of their existence. It was worse for women. There were hardly any jobs available and whatever work they could find paid only enough for them to survive. Their tasks in sweatshops were gruelling. They could be found tailoring, scrubbing, or making sacks, or matchboxes and picking hops.

All of these jobs were carried out without any regard for health and safety standards. Despite the working day being long, the pay was meagre. For seventeen hours of hard labour, a woman would earn about ten pence, minus the cost of materials. Desperation turned many women in Whitechapel toward prostitution. One account stated that they were so desperate that they would offer sex in return for a loaf of bread, or three pence. In some houses, children would be sent out of the house until after midnight while their mothers engaged in prostitution to make enough money for food. Some children would collapse from exhaustion or experience intense pain from chronic starvation. According to the Metropolitan police in October 1888, more than 1,200 prostitutes were working in the Whitechapel district alone. It was estimated that one out of every 16 women was involved in prostitution. For many, the sex trade was the only means of survival and income. With alcohol being comparatively cheap, both men and women took to drink. Drunkenness was rife and frequently led to violence. In these conditions, alcoholism became a common affliction.

Workhouses in the District

With origins tracing back to the Poor Law Act of 1388, workhouses were originally set up to offer accommodation and employment for those who could not support themselves. Whereas they were ideally meant for the able-bodied who were truly destitute, as the 19th century wore on they became refuges for the sick and elderly. Even for the women of Whitechapel, workhouses would have served as the most viable source of income and sustenance. But entering a workhouse meant they would be forfeiting the responsibility of their family. A mother could only keep her child with her as long as the child was under the age of two. Unlike the workhouses out of London, the workhouses in the East End had to compete for valuable space. As a result, the Whitechapel workhouses were often cramped. Despite the promise of food and shelter, most people would consider these workhouses as prisons.

Gender Difference at Work

Many scholars have used the Victorian era as an example of a period in which the gender roles were polarised. Marriage was one of the most significant events in a woman's life, leaving her highly dependent upon her husband and his income. Women rarely received work training or were given the opportunity to develop skills necessary for earning a living. Consequently, in the event that a woman had to support herself and her family, she had very limited employment options.

In a society where women were viewed as sexual objects, it followed that they would use their sexuality as a means of income in times of dire need. This simply meant prostitution.

Girls from underclass families would grow up with little or no education and be required to contribute to the family's income. This could mean being forced into labour at a young age. Those not able to find jobs had a bleak alternative. Most prostitutes started out in the profession by the age of 12, but some as young as nine would be coerced. Yet a large number of women during the era also regularly earned their living through paid labour. By 1851, a total of more than two million women and girls above 10 years of age were employed across the nation in a female population of over ten million. They formed at least 30 per cent of the entire labour force. From these numbers, it can be safe to assume that a portion of the female population in Whitechapel found work other than in prostitution.

Thousands of women from lower-class families became domestic servants for middle and upper-class homes. Toward the end of the 1800s, the city of London alone had a total of over 200,000 domestic servants, whereas the nationwide totalled about 905,000. Washerwomen and charwomen also made up a large majority of the female workforce during this time.

It is likely some of these women were Whitechapel residents. Yet the dilapidated conditions in the district combined with a high crime rate, drunkenness and high mortality, played a significant role in the rising numbers of prostitutes in the area.

Education

The economic status of women during the Victorian era was based on the family they were born into. Educational opportunities were extremely limited for any woman. Gender determined the freedom of education in those times. Women were not encouraged to study science, art, law, engineering, or physics. The common assumption was that only men were capable of learning these subjects. Women's education typically involved studying general literature, history and geography. It was designed so that they would have interesting yet noncontroversial conversation topics.

It was rare for a woman to go to university. They were told that studying could result in illness, as it was not in their nature. With this attitude toward education for women in middle- and upper-class families, the plight of women in working-class and underclass homes was desperate. They were starkly distinguished by their lack of education, which also meant fewer employment opportunities. Lower-class women in fishing towns made a living by preparing and selling fish or making and repairing fishing nets. Domestic service was a common option for lower working-class women or they found work as chambermaids, barmaids and waitresses. Some sold their wares such as flowers, oysters, or shrimps, on the street. Some turned to drink. Drunkenness in women was mostly recorded among the lower-class societies.

In many parts of the country, women's work was seasonal, so those who sold goods in the summer would have no means of income during the winter. Some were obliged to live on the charity of richer families, while others were dependent on relatives who were just as poor. A large number of the lower-class women would permanently descend to the underclass where they would be forced to resort to prostitution to survive. The upper sub-class of the lower class were families who were able to secure a slightly higher income and status by becoming shopkeepers, tradeswomen and domestic servants. With some education, young women of the upper lower class might get the chance to become governesses for richer families. Some lower-class families with money could even set up a business or school for their daughters.

Contrary to popular belief, businesses in some parts of the country were run by women. Printing, straw-hat making, and dress-making were quite popular among the upper working-class tradeswomen. They would run the business with their husbands and inherit it after his death, so several of the women from working-class families had a stable source of income.

Employment for the Working Class

Whereas women from middle- and upper-class families could live in luxury from the income of their husbands or fathers, working-class women often had to look for employment. Some needed a job to make ends meet, while others had to ensure the family's income in times of illness, injury, or sometimes death of their husband, who was the primary breadwinner. It was only toward the end of the Victorian era that workers' compensation was introduced. Before that, a woman had to either work to pay the rent, or stay at a workhouse in case her husband became too sick or injured to work.

In 1843, a government enquiry discovered that women traditionally handled the major tasks in agriculture, but toward the second half of the 1860s, agriculture work was no longer profitable, prompting more and more women to seek employment in industries and factories.

However, throughout the 19th century, domestic service was the single largest profession for women in the country. It was highly common for an unskilled young woman to become a servant for one of the middle or upper-class homes. During those days, there was no legislation regulating the hours and pay scale of domestic servants. An 1873 calculation showed that a housemaid's day would extend from 6am till 10pm. In between, she was allowed two-and-a-half hours to complete her meals and another hour-and-a-half for needlework. With four hours of rest, a housemaid of the time worked an average of about twelve hours every day. A female worker at a factory worked two hours shorter than a domestic servant. Moreover, factory work involved shorter working hours on Saturday and a holiday on Sunday. A housemaid would still be expected to work the usual hours even during the weekends.

Several women found employment in heavy industry, such as coal-mines and the steel industry, although when the Mines and Collieries Act of 1842 was implemented, women could no longer work underground. As the era wore on, changes in employment laws resulted in fewer numbers of female factory workers. While cities such as Birmingham, Leeds and Manchester saw the establishment of textile mills providing an important source of employment for women, the dwindling numbers of manufacturing plants in London meant job opportunities for women diminished by the end of the 19th century.

In the City of London, it was common for women to work for a wage from their home. They would spin and wind silk, wool, or other types of piecework to provide for the family. These tedious tasks paid very little and women had to work for as long as 14 hours to earn enough for survival. Many of the city's working-class households made a living by assembling and finishing furniture. These jobs paid relatively well in comparison to other available tasks. In particular, women were referred to as French polishers, completing the finish on the furniture. For the working-class women, the lowest-paying jobs included making matchboxes and sorting rags in rag factories. The rags, often riddled with fleas and lice were pulped and produced into manufacturing paper. Needlework was also one of the most popular occupations.

These home-manufacturing industries earned the name of 'sweated industries'. According to the 1890 House of Commons Select Committee, these industries were defined as work carried on for minimum wages through prolonged periods of time within unsanitary living conditions. Toward the end of the century, these workers could earn about one penny for one hour of work. Many women also earned a living by washing clothes at home, while some even worked as street vendors. They would bring in items like lavender, herbs, watercress, or flowers from the fruit and vegetable markets and sell them for a profit on the street.

In the flats of the slum districts, families would breed birds, rabbits, dogs and geese, and then sell them to the bird and animal markets. It was not uncommon for officials to find livestock, such as donkeys and cows in the cellars during housing inspections. Wages were based on gender and it was considered normal for a woman to get paid less for the same amount of work as a man. This is in spite of the fact that women were just as likely as men to be supporting a family. According to a government report in 1906, a woman working at a factory earned in old money an average of 11 shillings and 3 pennies for a week's work. On the other hand, a man would earn around 25 shillings and 9 pennies for the same work.

The Rise of Prostitution

During the 19th century, prostitution became a major concern for social and religious reformers. Most of the women who resorted to the profession were bound by economic necessity. The choice was bleak: starve and die, or engage in prostitution and survive. Some blamed the population explosion, while others blamed the women. In truth, a wide variety of factors contributed to the increase in the number of prostitutes everywhere and slum areas like Whitechapel became infamous. With the spread of venereal diseases, virgins were considered highly valued because they were deemed untainted. A large majority of prostitutes came from poor, lower-class families. Half were orphans. Without parental guidance and financial support, young girls were quickly forced into prostitution to earn a living. Some of the women also held on to their low wage jobs and worked the streets at night to make their ends meet.

Some prostitutes had been kidnapped at a young age and forced into the trade. For other women prostitution seemed to be the only viable income option, as they had to support illegitimate children – a woman having children out of wedlock at that time was considered as "unhireable" for any other type of work. Some women would see their entire life falling apart after the deaths of their husbands. Widows had to walk the street when distant male relatives inherited their entire fortunes and creditors began knocking on their doors. According to the inheritance laws, women were allowed to inherit only the money that went with her to her marriage. Most of the time, they would barely have enough to live on.

Being a courtesan or a mistress was one of the better fates of women during the era. Particularly for women in districts like Whitechapel, there was little or no hope of rising to a different class of society. Many found themselves in prison-like asylums, where they were expected to engage in hard physical labour. Some even landed in Lock Hospitals, which were designed for the treatment of venereal diseases and later developed into rehabilitation centres.

A small handful found refuge in reform houses like Charles Dickens's Urania Cottage. The focus was to help reform women in the sex profession and pave the path for their emigration to the colonies. It was not uncommon for a prostitute to marry her former client. Many of them would save up their earnings, so that they can switch to a different occupation and start a family. For the unfortunate ones, alcohol and opium became their main vices.

With the Ripper murders, the deplorable and inhumane living conditions of the poor became highlighted. They drew attention to how the underclass struggled to survive. Within the next two decades after the murders, a large number of London's worst slums were demolished. However, a series of puzzles remained unsolved. Was it the profession of those victims that made them the target of those crimes? Did their profession put them at a higher risk of becoming victims of such violent crimes?

Chapter 3

Violence Against Women

Violence Against Women

Cheap alcohol was easily available so drunkenness was rampant and was often closely followed by a violent crime. There were plenty of children pickpockets who roamed the streets, while women mostly shoplifted, while the sly conmen and "sharpers' targeted the middle and upper-class citizens of London. Housebreakers worked in teams to rob homes and shops, as well as warehouses. Muggers notoriously used violence – subduing people with chloroform-dipped handkerchiefs or tipping men's hats over their faces – to carry out their crimes.

The 18th century was a transitional period for England, which resulted in fewer crimes and protests, as well as the start of the modern police system with the Bow Street Runners. Society also went through a time of transition in terms of sexual equality and some historians noted that the sexes were more equal in the traditional rural agricultural community of this time compared to 19th century society. Yet despite this equality, there was a large gap between the rights of both sexes.

Women were still considered the "property" of their husbands or fathers. Even when it came to sexual crimes like rape, the loss of property was more of a concern than violence against women. However, women had it much easier during this period than in the years that would follow. The disadvantages faced by women in the industrial society were mostly consolidated during the latter parts of the Victorian era. Many experts on the Ripper murders see this as an element that played a role in the crimes.

Crime and Safety
in Victorian London

London was not a safe place during the early Victorian era. From Charles Dickens's *Oliver Twist*, we get an indication of what the city streets were like during the period – thieves from the East End slums turning young orphans into pickpockets and women battered to death in dark alleyways, or dingy rooms. We also see a lurid depiction of the East End slums in *The Nether World* by George Gissing, which described the people living there as despicable as their living conditions. But do these fictional depictions really define the facts?

According to Sir Robert Peel's biographer, Douglas Hurd, this was not the actual case in those days. He claims citizens could sleep easily at night after the new Metropolitan Police Force was introduced in 1829. This claim may have been supported by the records of police arrests as of 1856, which could be found in J. Ewing Ritchie's *The Night Side of London* (1858).

According to the reports, the total number of people taken into custody that year was 73,240 – 45,941 of them male. The report showed that 18,000 of the arrests were made owing to drunkenness and 8,160 were owing to unlawful possession of goods. A total of 7,021 people were apprehended for simple larceny, while 6,763 were arrested for common assault. Out of the total arrests made, 2,194 were for assaults on the police and 4,303 of the women were arrested for prostitution. A number of factors, however, suggest that these records only showed a fragment of the true crime status in Victorian London.

It was common for crimes to go unreported during those times. Many of the recruited "bobbies" were discharged for being drunk on duty, which added to the dwindling level of trust people had for their new police force. In the case of crimes like mugging and theft, victims felt it was useless to report the event to the police. Additionally, some victims would be too intimidated by their assailants or even embarrassed by the circumstances – for instance, their own drunkenness or involvement with prostitutes at the time of the crime.

A common ruse used by muggers involved luring men away from open public spaces with the help of prostitutes. Once the men were out of sight, the muggers would beat them up and take their valuables. Violence easily escalated to murder, and prostitutes themselves were at an increased risk of becoming the victims of such crimes. There are no known records of the total number of prostitutes who were strangled, butchered, or stabbed.

The city was so unsafe that it was unusual for a respectable woman to be seen on the streets after dark. Thieves, or muggers would throw nitric acid in a policeman's face if he appeared on the scene of the crime. As a result, the helpless were particularly at risk. Children might find themselves being dragged down dark alleyways where they were robbed. Pet dogs were sometimes kidnapped for ransom or even for their skins.

By the mid-19th century, "garrotting" created panic throughout the city. This involved muggers surprising the unwary by half-strangling them from behind while one or more accomplices stripped them of their fineries. Both big-time criminals and street hooligans indulged in crimes of different sorts. The 1880s saw a surge in gun crime and hardened burglars would go armed when carrying out their crimes. The open markets of London's East End, the railway stations, and the seedy districts of south London, were among the most crime-infested areas in the city. However, anyone could be the victim of a crime in any crowded or isolated area. An 1850 letter to The Times, which can be found in Dictionary of Victorian London by Lee Jackson, described a mugging near Regent's Park. According to the letter, the two assailants were fashionably dressed and began chatting with the victim about the weather. Later on, they were able to elude a policeman, as he believed they were just "gents" loitering about after a night in town. In Victorian London, Liza Picard wrote about an MP who, in broad daylight, was attacked and "garrotted" by two men in 1862. One of the men stole his watch while the other beat him. Changes and improvements in the Metropolitan Police Force helped create a safer London toward the second half of the 19th century. However, this did not eliminate knifing and mugging, as gangs of hooligans continued to prowl the streets in some areas and infanticide and domestic violence were still likely to go unreported.

Role of Gender in Crime

Crimes committed by women were likely to be fewer and different than those committed by men. Serious crime was mostly attributed to men, while sexual immorality was blamed on females. Most of the time, women were only accused of committing minor offences, particularly theft. The crimes committed by women were usually theft from shops, pick pocketing, receiving stolen goods, stealing from masters and employers, and stealing from lodging houses. Other common "female attributed" crimes included keeping a brothel, kidnapping, coining and childbirth-related offences. Only a small handful of females were charged for robbery, breaking the peace, sexual offences, or deception. These differences in male and female criminology were partly owing to the prescribed gender roles and occupations. Violence and aggression were expected from men, while prostitutes would steal from their clients, and housemaids from their masters. Men were more likely to steal from places of work.

Industrialisation and the Early Victorian Era

With crime rates constantly on the rise, the early 19th century was seen as a period of violence and degradation. Many working-class families were crowded into one-room flats in the slum districts. Prolonged exposure to inhumane and unsanitary living conditions resulted in brutalisation among factory workers and other working class men.

The poverty and indifference also impacted on sexual relations, according to the 1844 classic by Frederick Engels – *The Condition of the Working Class in England*. Engels gave a graphic description of the domestic situation in places such as Manchester. He said the husband worked all day long and maybe even the wife and elder children. Their work would be in different places, giving them the chance to meet only during the mornings and nights.

All would have the temptation to drink, which might have affected family life. It wasn't possible for the working man to escape from the family and his fatherly duties. According to Engels, this resulted in a series of problems in family life – domestic quarrels, neglect of children, and neglect of domestic duties. He stated that such situations were highly common in many working-class English homes. With no other means of recreation, the working class turned to sex and drink, which were usually carried out in excess. Some scholars pointed out that this excess could be associated with insecurity and poverty.

In the new factories that had been set up, young women found employment only to experience what we would refer to today as "workplace harassment". Employers reigned supreme over their employees, as they had all the leverage. In nine out of ten cases, harassment victims would fear showing resistance because of the threat of unemployment, which they could not afford.

Domestic Violence against Women

During the 19th century, "wife beating" was a common occurrence in many English homes. It was considered socially acceptable and was prevalent in both lower- and middle-class homes, as well as the homes of upper-class families.

Montagu Williams related in *Round London: Down East and Up West* that sometimes 12 or 14 women with bruised and bleeding bodies and faces would be seen waiting in the receiving-room of the London Hospital on a Saturday night. In nine out of ten cases, the injuries were inflicted by the husbands of the victims. Most domestic violence cases in the Victorian era were influenced by alcohol. Although Williams portrays "wife beating" as something that happens in lower-class households, there had been other reports of domestic violence even in higher-class homes. A mid-19th century English author, Caroline Norton, often wrote about the incidents of domestic violence in her own home. Her husband was a member of parliament who often engaged in "wife beating".

The perception of laws, domestic principles and religion during the period allowed men to justify their violence and dominance over their wives. It was commonly accepted that man is the ruler of all worlds, which contributed to the social acceptance of "wife beating". In the religious aspect, religious texts suggested that a woman should follow the lead of her husband in order to serve God with virtue. From this, society got the impression that men had the right to be in control over their wives. The use of physical force was not considered wrong as long as it involved a man disciplining his wife.

According to one of Caroline Norton's accounts, when Norton disagreed with her husband and defended another lady, he seized her by the nape and dashed her down on the floor. Her husband believed that with this action, he was keeping her "in line". Most of the laws during this era were favourable toward men's rights. They had the legal power over a majority of their wives' possessions, which included her wages and children, as well as any of her inheritance. In Wife Torture in England, Frances Power Cobbe describes that many women felt as if they were enslaved by their husbands. She wrote, "The whole relation between the sexes in the class we are considering is very little better than one of master and slave." While men were regarded by law as "persons", women's rights as independent "persons" were yet to be legally recognised. If a woman brought any property into her marriage, she lost it to her husband even after being divorced from him. She was not allowed to open a banking account and if married, had no right to end a contract without a legal approval from her husband. As a result of these property restrictions, it was next to impossible for a woman to escape from a failed marriage. There was no hope of exerting any control over her finances even if her husband was unwilling or unable to do so on her behalf. Legal and social reformers were increasingly focused on domestic violence and while in 1824, Britain's first animal-cruelty legislation was passed it was not until 1853 that women were granted legal protection from domestic abuse. That year that the Act for the Better Prevention and Punishment of Aggravated Assaults on Women and Children came into place. However, even this law did not impose a complete ban on violence by a man toward his wife and children. All it did was enforce a legal limit on how much force a man was permitted to use. One huge challenge that prevented the decline in domestic violence was convincing women to make use of the new law when their husbands battered them. An organisation was formed in 1843 to help with this cause, with the main focus on working class women. The organization worked toward notifying the authorities about the worst cases of domestic abuse.

In terms of the legal standing of women, things slowly began to change. While previously fathers were always given the custody of their children, the 1839, Custody of Infants Act put an end to that. Women gained a limited access to divorce with the passing of the Matrimonial Causes Act. However, this required a woman to prove that her husband was guilty of adultery as well as bigamy, cruelty, desertion, or incest. After amendments were made to this law in 1878, women had the right to file for separation on the grounds of cruelty. From then on, magistrates even began authorising protection for women whose husbands had been convicted of aggravated assault. In 1857, it became legal for a woman to seek divorce on grounds of violence. When the Married Women's Property Act was amended in 1884, it resulted in a major change in the legal status of women. It was recognised by legislation that a wife is not the property of her husband but a separate person.

The Morals of the Victorian Era

In the 1836 poem Porphyria's Lover by Robert Browning, we get a clear picture of social life and morals during the period. It reflects the agency of sexual violence in a society dominated by men but threatened by the independence of women. The narrator of the poem embodies the common sentiment of Victorian men – misogynistic and vengeful against strong-willed women. When Porphyria displayed her autonomy, her lover felt threatened and resorted to killing her in order to establish his dominance. The lover gets away with murder, while Porphyria faces condemnation for displaying her sexuality and asserting herself. The poem shows us the ideals and morals of society during those days, when sexual violence was considered as a necessary act for controlling rebellious women. Such was the injustice faced by women that in many cases sexual violence was not even seen as a criminal act.

Social reformers focused on reforming working-class society by withdrawing married women from work, so the women could concentrate on their domestic and motherly duties. This resulted in the isolation of the domestic sphere of working-class homes from the eyes of the public and also from the scrutiny of the new criminal justice systems. Although the state intervened with the aim of reforming and strengthening the family to become a self-regulating institution, it was at the expense of the identification of domestic violence.

Economic class also became a major hurdle in women's protection against domestic violence or sexual crimes. Caroline Conley wrote that women were expected to be submissive and obedient in order to "deserve" protection. This was usually reserved for women of middle-class society because the common assumption was that although women of the working class could be respectable, they did not possess the delicate aspects that were considered as feminine. She wrote, "The right to protection was based on the assumption that women were weaker, softer, and generally very different from the strong men who protected them."

It was the aim of religious leaders and middle class reformers to educate the working classes about notions of "respectability" and family life. While in the early 19th century, the working class was considered as dangerous and feared by the middle and upper class, the second half of the century was mainly spent on "reforming" the lower classes. By spreading the notions of moral education and reform, they aimed to develop a stable and united working class that was capable of providing a reliable workforce. Several efforts were made for this moral reform – improvements on public health and housing, free elementary education and development of Sunday schools. The working class started learning about what we would refer to today as "family values". It was also the aim of the police as well as evangelicals to provide spiritual guidance to the "fallen woman".

The "fallen woman" in the Victorian era was a woman who was married to one man but had sexual contact with another man. The expectation during those days was that women have sex with only their husbands, while it was perfectly acceptable for a man to have multiple sexual partners. Several examples can be seen in Victorian literature and art about women facing dire consequences for straying from their moral expectations.

In Thomas Hardy's *Tess of the d'Urbervilles,* we read about the story of a woman who was punished by her community because she lost her virginity before marriage even though the reason for that was rape. In *Anna Karenina,* Tolstoy talked about an adulteress meeting a tragic end and so did Flaubert in *Madame Bovary.*

The situation worsened with the 1864 first Contagious Diseases Act. If a woman was suspected of being "unclean" she was subjected to a genital examination. If she refused to get the examination, she could be thrown to jail for refusing. If she was diagnosed with an illness, she could be involuntarily confined in the hospital. This law was only applicable for women, giving social and legal activists a major rallying point. Activists argued that the disease prevention law was unfair to women and ineffective. Male policemen would perform the exams without any medical training or knowledge. As a result, a woman was easily diagnosed with a disease based on inaccurate evidence or no evidence at all. Moreover, the exams were both painful and humiliating for the woman being examined.

Such were the morals of the people during those days, that women – particularly from the lower class – held the lowest place in society. They had no say in even the most important decisions concerning them. Even if a woman received brutal beatings from her husband, social norms justified this act as a way of "disciplining" her. It would be unwise to jump to conclusions and say that men violently attacked women for no good reason. However, the perception is that women were highly susceptible to become victims of domestic abuse if they ever dared to contradict their husbands.

Reform, Crime, and Sexual Violence

As religious leaders and social campaigners worked toward reforming working-class families, the position of women changed and this was reflected in the public sphere. Instead of putting their family lives on full display to the public, they began to keep things more private. With this, there were also several changes in the way society saw domestic violence.

Historian Joanna Bourke wrote that violence by men toward their wives and children was not random, but was subject to a certain set of rules and rites. There was a sharp distinction between what was considered "legitimate" and "illegitimate" when it came to domestic violence. A man had to show that he was the "boss" of the house for him to be considered as a man. On the other hand, excessive violence could drag his reputation down to the ground. "Legitimate" violence rules created some peace within neighbourhoods. From the third quarter of the 19th century, the crime rates dropped down to a significant extent.

In London, there were 800 records of aggravated assaults for the year 1853 and only 200 for the year 1889. This downward trend continued even as the 20th century dawned. However, historians still doubt whether or not this decline meant a change in the level of violence. In her study about "wife beating" in London, Nancy Tomes mentioned that there were highly visible signs of the actual beating. It was not unusual for neighbours to watch or even participate in the personal quarrels of others.

These neighbourly interventions were mainly in an attempt to moderate or prevent a beating. If it were likely that a fight might be starting, they would watch the couple closely. The surveillance was usually followed or accompanied by reprehension toward the husband and his actions. It was common for the community to help the wife by offering her shelter or nursing her after a beating. By removing domestic violence from the streets, the reform movements put an end to the communal surveillance. As a result, wives were still beaten behind closed doors, and domestic abuse became increasingly invisible to the eyes of the public.

This could be one of the reasons why actual reports of domestic violence decreased in number during the latter half of the century. Tomes wrote: "The decline may be an artifact of the erosion of community control over individual behaviour. As working-class families moved to larger homes in suburban areas, their violence may have become more private. Neighbours could not interfere as easily in family violence that they could neither see nor hear."

She also stated that women were less likely to seek help as victims of domestic violence if the beating was viewed as a shameful act. Communities moved toward a stable patriarchal family system centred around "domesticated manliness", which was less aggressive than the earlier period. Emphasis was laid on the husband being a provider and a protector. Like her middle-class counterparts, the working-class woman began withdrawing herself from the world of work and focusing on her household duties.

For a decline in violence toward them, women had to pay with submissiveness and dependence. They increasingly embraced the middle-class notion that women needed "natural protectors" because they were weak, fragile, and passive. Society was yet to accept that both the victim and the offender should have legal equality. Violence in the domestic sphere of a family became less and less visible to the public eye, and without public surveillance, the victim increasingly became the only witness of the assault. In working-class communities, crime control began revolving around publicly visible crimes. As society began seeing family life as "private", any intervention by outsiders could be considered as a violation of privacy. However, the measures that had been taken by reformers to create a more stable family, took a turn to reinforce the invisibility of domestic violence.

The preservation of the family increasingly displaced the question of criminalisation, even if violence occurred. In his study about middle-class and working-class family conflicts, James Hammerton criticised the dependence on court statistics that showed a decline in domestic violence. Hammerton wrote that it would be unwise to rely too much on those statistics because the courts had become courts of summary conviction and conciliation. The Matrimonial Causes Act on 1878 allowed a woman to file for separation and maintenance allowances if her husband was convicted of aggravated assault.

However, the local magistrates started taking on a paternalistic role, with an eagerness to intervene. They would make attempts to convince the wife to forgive, and the husband to reform, so that the family could unite again. Their intention was to avoid the division of the family's meagre economic resources. It was common for magistrates, probation officers, court clerks and police court missionaries to consider themselves as "marriage menders". This played an important role in the decline of domestic violence reports.

In a society where women had the last say in every decision, there were still evident hints of misogyny and the belief that women were a weaker sex. If any woman strayed from the conventional feminine ideals accepted by society, she was quickly labelled as "loose" or deviant. The 1888 Ripper murders took the city by storm and greatly impacted the Victorian views of women and their social standing.

Since the murders were accompanied by sexual mutilation, the media and the public alike were engulfed in ideas about unchecked male sexual fantasies. In the chapters that follow, we will be taking a closer look at the victims along with the Ripper's modus operandi. There are hundreds of theories and assumptions about the killings all asking the same questions. Did the killer have a particular hatred towards women, or was he just influenced by the social and cultural norms regarding women's sexuality?

Chapter 4

The First Whitechapel Murder

The First
Whitechapel Murder

The brutality of the attack on Emma Elizabeth Smith shocked the nation. She staggered away from the scene and was able to give police an account of what happened before she died of her injuries. She had been beaten, raped and – worst of all – she had a blunt object thrust into her vagina, which ripped her perineum and caused heavy bleeding.

The murder of prostitute Emma Elizabeth Smith caused an uproar in London and her case was closely followed by the press. The killing took place in the impoverished, dank and largely neglected area of Whitechapel where there was a large migrant population, abject poverty and overcrowding. Emma Elizabeth Smith, like most women of her generation living in Whitechapel, had taken the only paid work available to her – prostitution.

Many prostitutes were attacked or died under suspicious circumstances in Whitechapel and the East End, but no one took heed until Emma Elizabeth Smith died. So what makes her so important? Why does she feature so prominently in the lore of Jack the Ripper? Why do Ripperologists study her so intensely?

It is because her murder shone a light on the conditions of prostitutes and the population in general in Whitechapel. Her murder forced the police to open their file on the Whitechapel killings that ultimately would chronicle all the moves of Jack the Ripper. Although much of it does not exist anymore, the file on the Whitechapel murders put the world in dreadful awe of the Ripper.

Many believe that Emma Elizabeth Smith was not one of the Ripper's victims, yet the sheer brutality of her death has stopped many from writing her off as just another who suffered a gang attack. She is definitely not considered as one of the Canonical Five – five murders that can be definitely linked to each other and the Ripper. However, she is possibly the Ripper's first known victim not to die instantly. What makes her intriguing and such an enduring subject of study, is her mysterious past.

The Background of Emma Elizabeth Smith

What is definitely known is that Emma was a prostitute from Whitechapel. But, as is the case with many records related to the Whitechapel murders and Jack the Ripper, most of the files and documents on her are missing. Before they could be sent to the Public Records Office, the papers were lost from the Metropolitan Police archive. Some were taken away, some were discarded or mislaid and others just vanished.

Emma Smith is particularly beguiling as her life was a mystery even to her closest friends. She made sure she hid her past from everyone she knew. Friends recalled that she always dodged their questions into her background with vague responses. Even the day of her birth is not known, but she was believed to be forty-five years at the time of her death in 1888.

Ripperologists know that she was living in a lodging house at 18 George Street, Spitalfields. This street is now known as Lolesworth Street. Records suggest that she once enjoyed a comfortable family life and was possibly born or married into substantial wealth before becoming a widow. How she fell to such lows and what forced her to become a prostitute in probably the worst place in London remains unsolved.

Notes taken by Detective Edmund Reid survive, which speak of a son and daughter that she claimed to have, living away from her in the Finsbury Park area of North London. She repeated this to her friends and acquaintances too, but she never disclosed with whom they were staying or how old they were. Emma never mentioned them by name although she often lamented that they should help her out.

Her friends and acquaintances kept her in high regard, which was extremely rare for a woman in her circumstances.

According to another detective, Walter Drew, she had broken away from all the people she knew from her past and had been a widow and prostitute for about a decade. Detective Drew found some clues why she was treated with more respect than other prostitutes. He noticed that this often unruly woman had an air of the upper class about her in the way she spoke, hinting that she could have once been a privileged woman. Whenever she was asked why she left her previous life completely, she would say, "They would not understand now any more than they understood then. I must live somehow." Her stories about her background were, however, filled with inconsistencies. She also told people that she left her husband and cut off all contact from him in 1877.

Emma followed a strict daily routine. She would leave her lodging house every day between six and seven in the evening, solicit customers at night, and return to her lodgings in the small hours of the next morning. Like most other prostitutes in London, she was a drunk, often in brawls and covered in cuts and bruises. Aggressive, loud-mouthed and violent, her general disposition has led many Ripperologists to believe her attitude may have gotten her in trouble with the Whitechapel gangs and pimps.

After her attack she had managed to stagger away to get help while bleeding profusely, and was even able to describe what happened to the police before she died. The extent of her injuries shocked the police into action and a nation into collective fear. However, the fact that she was raped makes most doubt that she was one of the Ripper's early victims. Unlikely for the police at that time, they actually opened a case for Emma Elizabeth Smith and followed every lead into her murder. But to no avail.

How Emma was killed

Here, it might be helpful to detail how Jack the Ripper stalked his victims and killed them. It might explain why there is so much confusion around the murder of Emma Smith. Ripperologists have come to certain conclusions about the method of the Ripper's murders and his signature style. With the Canonical Five and his earlier victims, he always struck in the early hours of the morning when the streets were empty and most people were asleep. It meant there were no witnesses and he could carry on without the fear of being interrupted.

Experts observe that he seemed to kill only during the weekends – from Friday to Sunday. He seemed to keep his murderous ways at bay during the weekdays, and there are suggestions that he had a full-time job. The Ripper followed a pattern with his victims. He would strangle them first, lay their body on the ground, and cut the throat starting with the side facing away from him. This allowed him to drain much of the victim's blood without being sprayed, then he would begin eviscerating the body.

The knife wounds on the victims and their directionality suggested that he was right-handed. As his organ removal methods were clean and precise, detectives believed that he was a surgeon, or someone with some medical experience. Another account of the Ripper's style had him apparently choosing a victim and stalking her. Once it was dark and secluded enough, he would grab her from behind and hold her, while slashing her throat. He would then supposedly move the victim to a quieter place to start mutilation. He would cut open the abdomen of the victim, remove organs such as the kidneys, and severely mutilate the genital area. He would also mutilate the victims' faces.

All of his victims were killed this way except for one. The brutality of his attack and his subsequent mutilation of their bodies, especially the genital area, first connected him to the murder of Emma Elizabeth Smith. He preyed solely on drunken prostitutes and his modus operandi showed anger and particular rage at women, although there was no indication of sexual assault or sexual activity on the women before they were murdered. Emma Smith was raped, which cannot clearly connect her to Jack the Ripper. However, here are the circumstances on the night she was attacked – 2nd April 1888, a Monday Bank Holiday. Emma Smith left her common lodging house at George Street in Spitalfields at 7pm as usual and she went to her usual area to solicit customers in the Whitechapel area late into the night. Margaret Hayes, who lived with her in the lodging house, reportedly last saw Emma at 12:15am. According to her, Emma appeared to be talking to a man wearing a dark suit with a white silk handkerchief wrapped around his throat. He was of medium height and of obvious wealth. They were standing together and talking to each other at the corner of Burdett Road and Farrance Street in Limehouse. Although police took note of this, the man appeared to play no part in her death.

Most of the details from that night came from Emma herself. She told the police she was in a drunken state and while walking past St Mary's Church on her way back to the lodging house at around 1:30am she realised that three men were coming towards her. Alarmed, Emma decided to cross the road but when she reached Osborn Street, she said that they attacked her, robbed her and then brutally raped her.

One of the attackers – and some reports say there were four men – was just a teenager of about 19, she said. The attackers thrust a blunt object into her vagina, which ripped her perineum, causing heavy bleeding. After robbing her, they left her to die on the streets. Bleeding profusely, she managed to get up and walk back alone to her lodgings. To absorb the blood and to halt the bleeding, she had taken off her shoulder wrap and placed it between her thighs. Mary Russell, the house deputy at the lodging house and another lodger, Annie

Lee, took Emma to the London Hospital on Whitechapel Road against her wishes.

Along with her other injuries, her face was badly bruised and her ear was cut off. At the hospital, she was treated by house surgeon George Haslip. With astounding strength, she managed to fight unconsciousness long enough to give a detailed account of her attack. She fell into a coma soon afterwards and died after four days on 4th April 1888.

Other facts that we know about the attack on Emma Elizabeth Smith was that she reached her lodgings between 2am and 3am. Dr Haslip determined that the blunt object pushed forcibly into her vagina was probably a stick. According to Mary Russell, when they were on their way to the hospital, they passed the Taylor Brothers' Mustard and Cocoa Mill; it was then when Emma disclosed she was attacked opposite the mill. The mill was located on the corner of Brick Lane and Wentworth Street.

Not the First Victim

Emma Elizabeth Smith may have been the first victim of the Ripper's who died from her injuries rather than instantly, or she may not have been his first victim. It is well-known that serial killers start small before going in for the big kill. It is

An illustration depicting the discovery of one of the victims of the Whitechapel murders, 1888.

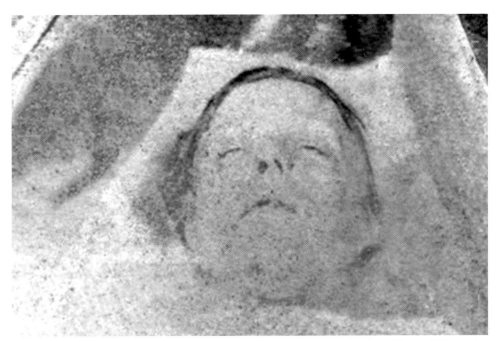

A picture from Scotland Yard of the body of Mary Ann Nichols, victim of Jack the Ripper, 1888.

A depiction of Police Constable Neil discovering the body of Mary Ann Nichols in Buck's Row, Whitechapel, 1888.

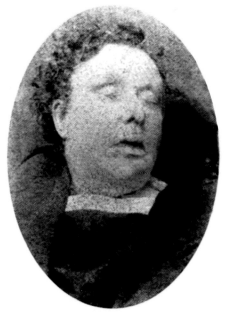

A picture from Scotland Yard of the body of Annie Chapman, after she became another victim of serial killer Jack the Ripper, September 1888.

The backyard of 29 Hanbury Street, Spitalfields, where the body of Annie Chapman was found in the space between the steps and the fence, 8th September 1888.

THE FRONT OF 29, HANBURY STREET.

An illustration of Hanbury Street that was released after the body of Annie Chapman was found in the early morning by Davis, a carman, 1888.

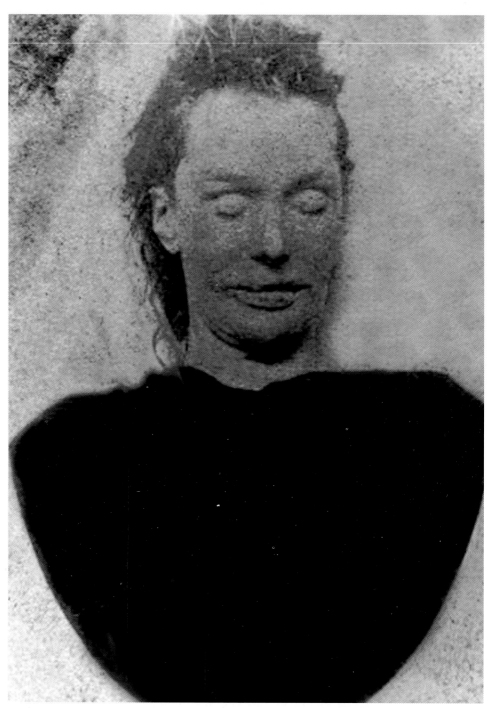

A picture released by Scotland Yard of the body of Elizabeth Stride, victim of Whitechapel killer Jack the Ripper, September 1888.

An illustration of the court in Berners Street, Commercial Road, Whitechapel, where the body of Elizabeth Stride was discovered by Lewis Diemschitz, a jeweller, 30th September 1888.

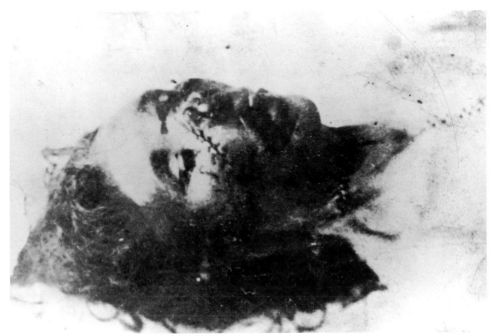

A close-up picture from the police archives showing the cuts to the face of Catherine Eddowes, one of the victims of Jack the Ripper, 1888.

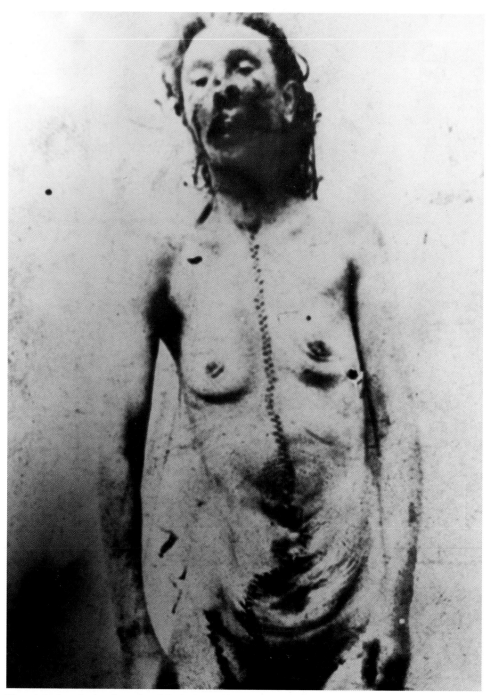

The stitched-up body of murdered Catherine Eddowes, the fourth victim of Jack the Ripper, following her post-mortem, 1888.

An on-the-spot sketch of the body of Catherine Eddowes, made by Dr F. Gordon Brown in Mitre Square, Aldgate, at first light, 1888.

An illustration of Catherine Eddowes who was murdered in Mitre Square, London, 30th September 1888.

An illustration depicting the graffiti that was found written in chalk on a wall in Mitre Square, following the murder of Catherine Eddowes; 'The juews are the men that will not be blamed for nothing.' 30th September 1888.

A police sketch of Mitre Square in Aldgate in 1888 drawn at the time to aid their investigation into the Ripper murder of Catherine Eddowes, 1888.

quite possible that his first few attacks were not brutal enough to kill the victims. Moreover, he would have taken time to perfect his modus operandi, allowing the first few victims to survive.

In the Jack the Ripper lore, three names stand out prominently as his first victims. These three victims are named 'Fairy Fay', Annie Millwood and Ada Wilson. If these three women were truly his first victims, it means that he had started attacking women in 1887. Moreover, there could have been many more victims who never came forward. However, Ripperologists dispute that Fairy Fay was a victim.

Jack the Ripper was rich copy for newspapers and when the news of the murders broke out, they dominated all coverage. In a bid to capitalise on the gruesome events, some newspapers often reported details and information without making any background checks. This is where the story of Fairy Fay emerged. It was claimed that there was a victim about twelve months before Annie Millwood and Ada Wilson were attacked, making Fairy Fay the first victim of the Ripper. The story was picked up by the Daily Telegraph and they ran with it.

The date of her death was reported to be 26th December and the location where she was found was said to be around Wentworth Street and Osborn Street. The Daily Telegraph reported that the victim was brutally attacked and had a blunt object thrust into her vagina. The woman was never identified hence she was named Fairy Fay. Yet there are no records of such a crime occurring, and it appears the Fairy Fay murder was a figment of a reporter's imagination. The fact that details of her murder so closely resembled that of Emma Elizabeth Smith, indicates that someone spun the story to spread more fear in London. They were both murdered on or near Osborn Street or Wentworth Street, they both had foreign objects forcibly thrust into their bodies, and they were both attacked in the early hours of the morning.

On the other hand, the story of Annie Millwood being a Ripper victim has some plausibility. She could have been a victim of his early days when he was unable to make a kill. Here's how her story goes: In the early hours of the evening of 25th February 1888, a middle aged woman was brought into the Whitechapel Workhouse infirmary with severe and several knife wounds to her lower torso and legs. She was later identified as Annie Millwood, a poor and destitute woman living in a lodging house.

Annie was 38 years of age when she was attacked and the widow of Richard Millwood, a soldier. Unlike Emma Elizabeth Smith, she was not soliciting at the time of her attack. Fortunately, her wounds were not as severe as those of Emma, and she was able to recount her assault clearly. She told the police she was attacked by a complete stranger with a clasp knife he took from his pocket. There were no witnesses to the attack. She appeared to recover from her injuries and was sent to the South Grove Workhouse. Ten days later she was back in the infirmary, having collapsed and died on 31st March 1888. After an inquest into her death, it was settled that she died of natural causes that were aggravated by her recent injuries.

Ada Wilson was the next supposed victim of Jack the Ripper. She claimed to be a seamstress – a profession that prostitutes used as a euphemism. On 28th March 1888, she was about to retire for the night when there was a knock on the door of her house in Maidman Street, Mile End. Ada opened the door to see a stranger who she later described to be around thirty years of age and of medium height (about 167.6 cm). The man demanded money and made it clear that if she refused to hand over any money she had only moments to live. When Ada refused the man drew out a clasp knife and stabbed her twice in the throat. Ada's screams were heard by her neighbours and they rushed out of their houses to help her. Fortunately, they also sought medical assistance, and a Dr Wheeler of Mile End Road was able to attend to Ada and dress her wounds at her house.

She was taken to the London Hospital on his orders. No one believed that she would survive the attack, let alone make a full recovery. However, Ada proved them all wrong and was released from the hospital on 27th April 1888.

Ada Wilson was unlike other Ripper victims, as not only were her neighbours able to help her, but there was also a witness. Rose Bierman, another resident in the house, rushed to the door when she heard screams and found Ada, partially clothed and bleeding from the throat, crying. Rose saw a young, fair man rushing out the door. Ada said the man wore light-coloured trousers, a soft felt hat with a wide brim and low crown and a dark coloured coat. His face was sunburnt and he had a fair moustache.

Rose found two constables outside the Royal Hotel and reported the attack to them immediately. The attacker managed to disappear and evade capture. As there was so much publicity around the Fairy Fay and Annie Millwood attacks, the police and the press followed every lead and angle. This invariably led to her being connected to the other attacks in Whitechapel and being linked to Jack the Ripper, although there was little evidence to substantiate these claims. Moreover, her attack had nothing in common with the attack on Annie Wilson, save for the clasp knife being used to stab the victims. And both these attacks most certainly had nothing in common with that of Emma Elizabeth Smith's.

'Fingers Freddy'

Just when everyone thought that the case of Emma Elizabeth Smith could not get more mysterious, out popped a shady character nicknamed 'Fingers Freddy'. This angle was first revealed in 1972 by Superintendent Arthur Butler, who wrote about the connection in his articles for The Sun newspaper.

According to Butler, Fingers Freddy was a street showman who enthralled crowds with magic tricks while his accomplices picked the audience's pockets. Emma Smith was one of his accomplices and he was also her protector, or pimp. Superintendent Butler also suggested that Emma Smith and Fingers Freddy knew the Ripper who was actually a woman.

According to Butler, the Ripper, who in his story was Jill the Ripper, was an illegal abortionist who lived and worked in the Whitechapel area. He assumed that Emma Smith and Fingers Freddy planned on blackmailing and extorting money from 'Jill', without knowing that she was the one who attacked the women. Emma Smith was attacked and died from her injuries. Whereas Fingers Freddy simply disappeared.

Who killed Emma Elizabeth Smith?

Before we can get to who attacked and killed Emma Elizabeth Smith, a little context is necessary. The fact that her murder made it to the front pages of all the newspapers is quite astonishing. Whitechapel, in those days, was probably the worst area to live and work in. In the 19th century, Jews who were exiled from their own countries fled to London. With no work and no means to support themselves and their families, many gravitated to the East End.

Londoners were suspicious of the massive influx of immigrants and there was much bad feeling. Once it was revealed that there was a serial killer loose around the Whitechapel area, anti-Semitism grew, as people believed that the murderer was possibly one of the immigrants.

There is no concrete evidence as to who Jack – or Jill – the Ripper was. Also Emma Elizabeth Smith described being attacked by three men. There is no record that Jack the Ripper had accomplices or was ever part of a gang. This coupled with the fact that she was raped when she was attacked, indicates that she was most probably attacked by her protectors and pimps.

The canonical victims showed no signs of sexual abuse. Also, the Ripper stabbed his victims and slashed their throats. Emma Elizabeth Smith was beaten up in a way that was inconsistent with the Ripper's modus operandi. As a result of all these inconsistencies, most modern Ripperologists believe that Emma Smith was not killed by the Ripper. They think that she was most probably attacked by one of the 'high rip' gangs that patrolled the Whitechapel and East End areas those days and controlled the prostitution business. As with modern-day prostitutes, most women were under the control of pimps and forced to pay protection money. Any disobedience was met with severe punishment. This could have been the case with Emma Elizabeth Smith. The sexual nature of her attack most certainly indicates she was attacked by a protection gang. It is quite possible that she picked a fight or dared to defy her pimps, who then proceeded to rob and attack her. The fact that they left her to die on the street rather than killing her shows that they wanted to send a message to the other prostitutes in the area, of the punishment that awaited them if they stepped out of line.

Chapter 5

Martha Tabram

Martha Tabram

Martha Tabram had five wounds inflicted on her left lung, two on the right lung, one on the heart, five on the liver, two on the spleen and six on the stomach. With a total of 21 wounds , the ferocius nature of Martha's murder sent a chill down everyone's spine. They realised that some diabolical force, in the form of a human being, was at work.

Martha Tabram is one of those women whose life is a classic example of how a working-class person in Victorian England can see their world collapse. Suffering from a long-standing drink problem, she was forced into prostitution in middle age owing to extreme poverty.

Her ordinary and sad life would have been of no special significance, but for the circumstances of her death. Her body, gruesomely mutilated, was found in the George Yard Buildings in a dark alleyway of Whitechapel in the early hours of 7th August, 1888. Her murder is a case in study for Ripperologists who to date debate if she was the first real victim of Jack the Ripper.

From the Beginning

It is on a bright spring day on 10th May, 1849, that Martha
Tabram is born as Martha White to Charles Samuel White,
a warehouse worker, and Elisabeth Dowsett. They lived in
Southwark, an area in London south of the Thames. She was
preceded by four siblings – Henry, Stephen, Esther and
Mary Ann.

In 1865, when Martha was sixteen, her parents separated
after a long history of domestic troubles, the kind common in
working-class society of those times. The next blow came
hard and quickly the same year with the sudden death of her
father late on an October evening after a supper of bread,
butter and beer. She was with her mother and older sister
Mary Ann, who had been visiting him. He was fifty-nine, and
had been ill for a few months. It was stated that he died a
natural death. One doctor who called to look at him
previously hinted at the possibility that the grief of separation
swallowed him completely. Charles was unable to bear being
separated from his wife.

A New Start

Martha lived with Henry Tabram, a packer in a furniture
warehouse. He was a short man with grey hair moustache,

and an imperial beard; he was always well dressed and well turned out. They were married at the Trinity Church in St. Mary's Parish in the Christmas of 1869, when Martha was twenty. The couple moved to 20 Marshall Street, which was close to the house where she was born. In the same year, 1871, she gave birth to her first child, a boy who was named Fredrick John Tabram. Charles Henry Tabram, her second son, was born in December the following year.

When Martha took to alcohol is not clear, but her marriage ended when Henry left her in 1875 owing to her drinking. By this time, she was suffering from alcohol related fits. When Martha drank, everything, including her husband and two young boys, receded into the background. Women drinking as boisterously as men was an accepted fact in the East London of those times. Alcohol was often the only respite from an intolerable life.

One person who knew her said Martha was one of those people who would prefer an alcoholic drink to a cup of tea. It was not an easy life for a woman left to her own devices in those times, although she was one of the few lucky women who continued to get support from their husbands. Henry continued to give her money each week for food and lodging. That, without doubt, was spent on alcohol. Driven by her compulsion to drink, she even started to accost Henry on the street, pestering him for more money, invariably creating a drunken racket.

Martha Turner

Henry Tabram stopped providing for Martha when he found out that she was living with another man, Henry Turner, who was in carpentry. He was completely unlike Tabram in habits and appearance. He was a short man, always dirty and shabbily dressed. He too sported a slight moustache and an imperial beard. The couple were together intermittently for over twelve years. Martha would often come back home late at night and sometimes disappear altogether. Confronted by Turner she would blame it on alcohol and the resultant fits that would often take her to the police station. Whether this was true, Turner did not know. What he did know was that he had seen Martha have fits while inebriated.

The Year of 1888

Martha, now thirty-nine, and Turner were managing their lives as best as they could in the circumstances. In 1888, Turner was unemployed and the couple had to resort to selling small articles and trinkets on the streets. They lived together for a period of four months at 4 Star Place on Commercial Road, Whitechapel, which belonged to a Mrs Mary Bousfield. Having fallen on hard times when they could not even manage a meagre rent, they left the place without notice in July 1888.

Turner, in disappointment with Martha, abandoned her to live separately at a working men's home on the same street. Martha had no option but to join the hundreds of prostitutes hanging around in the streets and alleyways to solicit men for as little as four old pennies. These 'four-penny knee-tremblers' paid for women's lodging in the common houses that offered a bed for people who could not afford the rent for a place of their own.

Death was easy to come by for women like Martha, but the circumstances of her demise not only shocked the neighbourhood, but the nation with. Turner met Martha for the last time on 4th August. She was roaming aimlessly and had nowhere to go. Overcome by pity, he gave her a shilling for old times sake to buy some trinkets for hawking. Whether she did that cannot be known, but there is a high possibility that the money was spent at the nearest pub.

6th August, a Bank Holiday

Martha knew that the 6th August, a Monday and a Bank Holiday in London, would prove to be profitable and decided to enjoy it by celebrating with Mary Ann Connelly, another prostitute popularly known as 'Pearly Polly'. They went drinking at pubs in Whitechapel, including the Two Brewers and White Swan on the High Street. At one point, they were joined by two soldiers, one a corporal, the other a private, and continued on their spree.

This continued until 11:45pm, when both Martha and Connelly went their separate ways to have sex with the men. Dark, isolated alleyways, and nooks and corners were the only places that these hasty acts could take place with any privacy. Connelly saw Martha go towards George Yard, which was a narrow alley that connected Wentworth Street and Whitechapel High Street, before disappearing in the dark folds of Angel Alley on the opposite side. This was the last time that anyone saw Martha alive. Next we know, her body was found brutally mutilated and murdered on the first-floor landing of the George Yard Buildings.

7th August, George Yard Buildings

The George Yard Buildings were converted into low-cost residential apartments for the working classes from a defunct weaving factory. Residents of the buildings gave their testimonies at the hearing held for the murder of Martha Tabram. A Mrs Hewitt, said she was suddenly awoken by shrill cries of "Murder!" sometime after midnight, but thought it only a minor disturbance and went back to sleep.

Elizabeth and Joseph Mahoney, a married couple, had been out with friends. The lights were out at this time of the night, and the dingy building was in darkness. They remembered climbing the stairs to their flat at around 1:50am, but did not notice anything amiss.

Elizabeth went out to arrange for some supper, and returned in ten minutes, and again did not see or hear anything suspicious. Meanwhile, outside the building, Police Constable Thomas Barrett was patrolling the area. He noticed a young man in a Grenadier Guardsman's uniform loitering on Wentworth Street, on the north end of the building. It seemed suspicious to him, especially at 2am in a completely deserted place with not another soul in sight. The Guardsman said he was waiting for a "chum who went off with a girl". The two men then parted and Barrett continued with his patrolling.

At 3:30am, cab driver Alfred George Crow returned home to the building after an exhausting day. In the darkness, he saw a body on the first floor landing. He did not give it much thought as it was common for homeless vagrants to seek shelter there. He continued to his own flat and woke up late in the morning after a good night's sleep. The day is about to break and a little light penetrates the dark interiors of the George Yard buildings. John Saunders Reeves, a dock labourer, leaves his flat at 4:40am to get to work. Coming down the stairs, he approached the first floor landing and froze with the sight of a woman's body sprawled in a pool of blood. He fetched the police. PC Barrett, who was still on duty, came back to the George Yard Buildings. Shocked, he sent for Dr Timothy Robert Killeen to examine the body. At 5:30 in the morning of 7th August, the bloody body of a plump middle-aged woman, 160 cm tall, with dark hair and complexion was officially declared dead.

It was Martha Tabram. Clothed in a long black jacket, dark green skirt, brown petticoat, stockings, black bonnet and a pair of spring-sided wornout shoes, her rounded arms and hands were neatly arranged at the side of her body with fists tightly clenched. The skirts she was wearing were raised up till the waist. Her legs were wide open, as if caught in the act of sexual intercourse. Even for an amateur observer, it was evident that this was an unusual murder.

The police released details of the appearance and clothes of the murdered woman to find out if a family was missing a person. There were a few claims that turned out to be misplaced and Martha was finally identified by Henry Tabram on 14th August. Owing to their estrangement for more than thirteen years, he was unable to shed any light on her murder. Mary Bousfield, who had been Martha's landlady at 4 Star

Place, confirmed her identity as Martha Turner, the name she took while living with Henry Turner.

The Post-Mortem

The official post-mortem was conducted by Dr Killeen, who revealed that the woman would have been killed approximately three hours before the body was first seen by him at 5:30am. That put the time of murder between 2:30am and 2:45am. There were no signs of any intercourse having taken place, which was odd given the position in which Martha was found. But what was shocking for the physician was that she had 39 stabbing wounds on her body. These included five wounds on the left lung, two on the right lung, one on the heart, five on the liver, two on the spleen and six on the stomach. This aspect of Martha's murder sent a chill down everyone's spine. Dr Killeen wrote in the report that there were 38 wounds, a result of stabs with an ordinary penknife wielded with the right hand. It was his analysis on the 39th wound that confused the police and provided a hot debating topic for the Ripperologists. He said that the 39th wound that was found on the chest bone was a result of an attack with something like a bayonet. He also noticed the skill with which the targeted mutilation was done and suggested the hand of a person was familiar with the human anatomy. It was very apparent that it was the work of a misogynist who had intended to mutilate and obliterate breasts, stomach, groin and genitals. Whether the motivation was a personal vengeance against Martha or something more intangible, was not established.

Metropolitan Police Investigations

Edmund Reid, a local inspector with the Metropolitan Police Force, H-Division Whitechapel, was put in charge of the investigation. Reid found himself investigating, perhaps, one of the most heinous murders of his time. There was great pressure to find the killer and he only had the testimonies of the residents of George Yard Buildings and that of Police Constable Barrett. The first obvious step that he took was to get PC Barrett to recognize the soldier he had spoken to near the Whitechapel buildings. Once he came to know about Martha and Connelly's outing on the night leading to her murder, the other was to get Connelly to identify the two soldiers the duo had been drinking with.

On the 7th August, PC Barrett was taken to the Tower of London to pick out the Grenadier. The identification parade did not serve the purpose. Barrett did not pick any of the soldiers lined up for him. But there were still some soldiers who had been on leave on 6th August and Barrett performed the identification exercise all over again on 8th August. He did point out one man but changed his opinion in favour of another soldier. His uncertainty was based on the fact that the Grenadier he had spoken to on the night did not have any badges except one for good conduct. Whereas, the first soldier he had picked did have some displayed on his uniform.

This second soldier was John Leary. He said he had been out celebrating the holiday in Brixton with another friend, Private Law. But they were not the soldiers who were entertained that night by Martha and Connelly. As Leary's version of the story goes, he and Law had missed each other at closing time, after which he went for a stroll. They finally met at The Strand at approximately 4:30am. They then had one last drink at Billingsgate to seal the night and headed towards the Tower. Private Law corroborated the same story when questioned separately and so were dismissed from further investigation because of their alibis and Barrett's own uncertainty.

The hopes of the police were still alive when they came to know that a corporal called Benjamin had been absent from service without leave on 6th August. He had returned immediately after the second identification parade. He was called for questioning promptly and then pardoned from further investigation when his father in Kingston confirmed his visit to him that night.

Amidst all these efforts, Mary Ann Connelly, aka Pearly Polly, had been missing, too. She had not come out to help the police or to give her statement. She was living with a cousin on Drury Street to get away from the scandal, but was ultimately found out and seen by the police on 9th August. In her statement, she was asked to identify the two men she and Martha had been with on the night of 6th August. She did not appear for the ID parade the next day and it was scheduled again for 13th August and the police made sure that she was present. How valuable she would be as a witness was uncertain. She came with alcohol on her breath and things did not look hopeful to the police.

She confidently said that none of the men at the Tower were the soldiers. She categorically told the officials that the men they had been out with were wearing white cap bands. Cap bands were only worn by Coldstream Guards, and Connelly was taken to the Wellington Barracks for yet another round of identification on 15th August. There, Connelly picked out two soldiers. The first suspect, named George, said he was with his wife on Hammersmith Road from 8pm onwards on the day and his wife corroborated this. The second soldier, called Skipper, was in the barracks after 11pm and an entry in the Guardhouse books validated the claim.

He did not leave the premise again that night. Both of them had sound alibis and Reid had to pardon them from further investigations.

Investigations now met an inevitable abrupt end. There were so many pieces missing in the mystery of the murder of Martha that Reid had to finally give up. There were no more witnesses and no other avenue seemed open to him.

Inquest and Judgement

George Collier was a deputy coroner for South-east Middlesex. He was in charge of the inquest into Martha Tabram's murder, conducted at the Working Lad's Institute on Whitechapel Road on 23rd August 1888. Residents of the George Yard Buildings came to testify. Dr Killeen and PC Barrett, along with Inspector Reid, also submitted their reports.

The case had to be dismissed on the grounds of insufficient evidence, lack of witnesses and the failure of the police to arrest a valid suspect. Collier gave the final verdict of murder by person or persons unknown. The detailed hearing of the case had quite an effect on the deputy coroner. He said that the crime was "one of the most dreadful murders any one could imagine," and that, "the man must have been a perfect savage to inflict such a number of wounds on a defenceless woman in such a way."

The newspapers had kept readers updated on the case, from the discovery of the body, to the details of the inquest. The East London Advertiser called the incident a mysterious murder that had surpassed many of its predecessors in its shameful brutality. The killing had shocked the nation and the confidence of the public regarding their safety was shaken. They had no idea that there were more murders to come.

A Ripper Victim?

There were five more murders that took place in the autumn of 1888. Though the culprit was never caught, the name that was to be remembered came into being because of letters sent to the police. Whether written by the real culprit, or not, can never be known, but they claimed responsibility for the murders. They were signed by Jack the Ripper.

Sir Melville Macnaghten became the chief of the Criminal Investigation

Department in 1889, a year after these murders had taken place. He published a memo containing his opinions about the cases in 1894. It is largely owing to his insistence that her death was the handiwork of a soldier, that Tabram was initially not included in the list of women killed by the Ripper. Sir Melville was never directly involved in the investigations and most of his theories were based on the opinion of certain police officers.

Martha's throat had not been cut, two weapons were allegedly used to mutilate her and she was not eviscerated. These were aspects that had consistently appeared in the case of the other five murders. But there are similarities with the other unfortunate women. Martha, a middle-aged prostitute from the Whitechapel area, was killed on an extended Bank Holiday weekend. Her neck, breasts, abdomen and the genital areas were terribly mutilated, and her body was found in an indecent posture. There are many theories that explain the use of two weapons in her case as compared to one that was used to kill the others. Many feel that being the first of his victims, there were bound to be dissimilarities owning to inexperience and the lack of a standardised modus operandi.

Philip Snugden's The Complete History of Jack the Ripper published in 2002, gives a detailed account of the incidents that led to Martha Tabram's murder and the investigations that followed. According to Snugden, Frederick Abberline (the chief investigative officer in the Polly Nichol's murder case), Sir Robert Anderson, Edmund Reid and Walter Dew believed the murder of Martha Tabram to be the manifestation of the madness of Jack the Ripper. It is only on the authority of Macnaghten, that future investigators discredited her murder in that light.

In Retrospect

Whether Martha Tabram has the distinction of being the first victim of the Ripper is a mystery. There are many schools of thought that go either way. The significance of the murder cannot be easily dismissed. Soon after, the mutilated body of Mary Nichols, another prostitute, was discovered just under half a mile away from the George Yard Buildings. The police, press and the public finally started to comprehend the reality of a possible serial killer in their midst. A review of newspaper articles at that point is enough to realise the madness of the times. In the end though, Martha Tabram, was as much a victim of a society in despair as a sadistic killer.

Chapter 6

The
Canonical Five

The Canonical Five

When Annie Chapman's body was found in a pool of her blood, her face was swollen and there were bruises on her face and chest, the size of a man's thumb. The position of Annie's hands and arms seemed to show that she tried to fight back before losing her life. On her outstretched hands, three of her fingers were badly bruised, missing the rings she normally wore.

Such is the notoriety of Jack the Ripper that many murdered or missing persons of the late 19th century have been tagged as his victims. However, there are only five that past the scrutiny of Ripperologists and seen as true Ripper victims. These are known as the Canonical Five.

Mary Ann Nichols

The first woman that Sir Melville Macnaghten recognised as victim of Jack the Ripper, was Mary Ann Nichols on Friday, 31st August, 1888. Mary Ann Nichols's life and brutal death is surrounded by mystery. Although researchers tried to get more details, much of the information is supposition based on information on the name of Polly Nichols as well as Mary.

During the observation of her body, her age was estimated at between 30 and 35; however, at the inquest, her father stated she was closer to being 44. He said she was often taken for younger, owing to her small, delicate features and her height – 5ft 2in. Mary had brown eyes and hair, high cheekbones, dark complexion and appeared "clean" despite being an alcoholic.

Her activities as a prostitute appeared to be by choice, as she had wilfully left her husband and children. She had not been put out and had not been denied restitution until husband, William Nichols, found she was walking the streets. The body of Nichols was found between 3:40am and 3:45am, lying in a footway at Bucks Row, approximately a ten-minute walk from Osborn Street. Quite drunk, she had headed east down Whitechapel Road at approximately 2:30am in search of customers to gain additional doss money, though she bragged to a friend that she had the money three times over and had spent it.

During Polly's time as a prostitute, services could be had for as little as a few pieces of bread. She was fully dressed; however, the men who found her noted that her skirt was pulled up further than was appropriate and out of respect, they corrected it. One of the men believed her to still be alive, but both were worried that they would be late for their shift, and for fear of losing their jobs they left the woman unattended, agreeing that they would send the first constable they saw to assist her.

The body was found by PC John Neil and she was declared dead by Dr Llewellyn at around 3:50am. According to the records, Nichols was dressed in a brown dress with a brown linsey frock, grey woollen petticoat, white chest flannel, white chemise, woollen stockings, a black straw bonnet trimmed with black velvet and men's boots. She had greying hair, poor teeth and bruises from what were believed to be altercations during her drunkenness. The doctor examining her was certain she had been attacked in that spot, though no nearby residents had heard anything during the night. She had bruises related to her death on her cheek and chin, her throat had been violently slashed from left to right, twice, probably while she was lying on the ground. There were no typical signs of struggle though other abuse with a blade was apparent.

The coroner determined that the weapon used to inflict the wound was a long sharp blade approximately 8in long. It had sliced clear through the windpipe gullet and nearly through the spinal cord; the woman's head was quite nearly separated from the neck. On the ground, the killer mutilated the body with a slice along her abdomen, jaggedly, from under the pelvis along the left of the stomach to just under the ribs to the right. In addition, there were two stab wounds on her private parts. This type of mutilation would be markedly different from the murders of the time.

Annie Chapman

In the early morning hours of 8th September, a Saturday in 1888, Annie Chapman's body was found in the backyard of 29 Hanbury Street, Spitalfields. The accounts on the finding of Annie's body are not clear, as there are two differing sets of accounts from police and inquest witness reports.

A witness had seen Annie speaking with a man prior to her death, although no one else heard anything until her body was found lying in the yard. Annie is understood to have been the second victim of Jack the Ripper, her body left out in the open for anyone to easily find, deep jagged wounds to the throat. This time the slashes in the stomach were followed by the removal of organs.

Annie Chapman was not a well woman. She was 5ft, stout, approximately 47 years of age and suffering from malnourishment, tuberculosis, and possibly syphilis. Her hair was brown and her eyes blue. She was missing two lower teeth, and while she was noted to have a taste for rum;

she was not listed as an alcoholic. She had three children with a husband she was estranged from for maybe two years prior to his death in 1886. Many people found that she was very sad about his death, the loss of one of her children, and the condition of a second.

She did not start into prostitution until after her husband's death, as he had been sending her an allowance of 10 shillings a week, fairly regularly and with crochet work and selling flowers she was kept well enough. After her separation from her husband, she had been known to live with two different men, and had been lodging in various places. Shortly before her death, Annie had been in altercations with other individuals, though how much as a result of drinking was unknown.

On more than a few nights she said she had felt ill and wanted to go to an infirmary. Some, if not many, of the bruises found on Annie were not new at the time of her death and the observation indicated that she was not eating well. She may well have been fatally ill with not long to live.

When Annie's body was found, it is said that her face was swollen and her tongue protruded just past her teeth, but not past her lips. There were bruises on her face and chest, the size of a man's thumb. Her legs were drawn up and her left arm lay across her left breast and her hands were raised, slightly, palms towards her upper body, appearing as if she had reached for her throat during the moments before unconsciousness struck. It is said that she had worn three rings that may have been forced from her fingers. She was found lying in a puddle of blood.

Although one witness report says the victim was killed in only minutes after an altercation, the observation suggested that the killer had ample time to use a sharp blade up to 8in long. He removed the intestines and part of the belly wall around the navel. The uterus was taken from the womb, much of the bladder was gone and the upper part of the vagina was missing. A flap of the abdomen was attached by a cord to the right shoulder and two more flaps from the lower abdomen were on the ground above the left shoulder surrounded by blood.

The way in which she was explored, and the tool used, indicated that the killer knew what they were doing. It was proposed that the culprit was a surgeon, or butcher. The markings on her body, suggested that she had been grabbed around the throat from behind, suffocating her, but the bruising did not suggest struggle or sexual assault.

Elizabeth Stride

The third victim recognised as the work of Jack the Ripper was Elizabeth Stride, also known as Long Liz. Liz was seen many times with a young man, just hours before her death. The description given by Police Constable William Smith was quite specific: The man was approximately 28 years of age, wearing a dark coat and deerstalker hat, and carrying a package wrapped in newspaper, some 6in by 18in.

Stride was also seen in an altercation with a man in the gateway where she would be found murdered. Israel Schwartz stated that he saw the woman thrown to the footway, and though she cried out it was not very loudly. In addition, there had been a second man on the opposite side of the street, smoking a pipe. Schwartz believed he was addressed by the first man as "Lispki". Liz was 45 at the time of her death, and described as being 5ft 3in tall, having a pale complexion, dark brown curly hair, grey eyes and was missing all her lower left teeth.

She had moved quite frequently over the years and had married once; to a man she ran a coffee shop with for a short while. It is reported that she had a stillborn child in 1865, but no other children. Her friend and the man in her life was Michael Kidney. She had been married to a John Stride but separated from him in late 1881, and he died in

1884. Long Liz, a prostitute, had been detained by police on numerous counts of drunken and disorderly conduct. On the night of her death, she was seen with a well-dressed man at least twice.

Elizabeth Stride was found dead nearly 7ft from the gates on the inside of Dutfield's Yard at 40 Berner Street, which is at the corner of Commercial Road and was known as Berner Street Club. It was nearly 1am on Sunday, the 30th September, 1888. She lay in a pool of blood, her left arm extended and her right arm over her stomach.

When she was found, her body was still warm, her knees were drawn up and a deep gash was torn across her throat. Her silk sash was frayed on the bottom edge by what appeared to be a sharp blade. No sign of struggle existed, her clothing was undisturbed. No murder weapon was located, and there were no footprints or blood marks at the scene.

In this particular case, it was not possible to determine if she was standing or lying on the ground when her throat was slashed. Other than the method of killing – a sharp blade across the throat that severed the windpipe – there were no other similarities to the other Ripper murders. Liz was not mutilated, but it was believed this was because the killer was interrupted.

Catherine Eddowes

Catherine Eddowes was next listed in the Canonical Five. Eddowes was also known as Kate Kelly, and was born on 14th April, 1842. She had a fierce temper, and was considered intelligent and scholarly. It was not believed that she had ever married, though she had three children with Thomas Conway, and when she left him two of the children went with her. Her daughter later married and moved around in an attempt to avoid her mother. Some of the reports suggested she was well liked, others suggested otherwise.

While her younger life was documented fairly well, including the activities of her large family and the work of her father, her adult life was less clear and her story revolves around her role as a victim of Jack the Ripper.

On the night prior to her murder, at 8pm, Catherine, aka Kate, was taken to Bishopsgate Police Station for drunkenness. Her time at the jail was to help her sober up. The police said she could leave once she appeared capable of tending to herself. She did not give her name at first, but upon release, she gave her name as Mary Ann Kelly. Her release was at 1am; 30 minutes later a commercial traveller named Joseph Lawende, along with two others, Harry Harris and Joseph Hyam Levy, would see her as they left the Imperial Club at 16–17 Duke Street. She was speaking with a man and her hand was on his chest. They described the man as around 30, around 5ft 7in tall, of medium build with fair skin and a moustache. He was wearing a loosely fitting jacket, with the general appearance of a sailor.

Catherine's body was found at 1:45am on Sunday, the 30th September, 1888, at Mitre Square, Aldgate, in London, by a policeman. Her clothing was disarrayed, and part of her apron was found on the ground near a wall in Gouldstone Street. On the wall in chalk writing were the words, "The Juwes are the men That Will not be Blamed for nothing." In order to prevent any possible hate crimes should the general public see it, the message was ordered to be washed from the walls immediately, even though later it was presented as evidence. It is uncertain if the person who dropped the piece of apron was also the person who wrote the message on the wall. Researchers found it an isolated case; no other messages were left at, or near, any of the other murder scenes.

Catherine was described as 5ft tall, with auburn hair and hazel eyes. She had a tattoo "TC" on her left forearm in blue ink, possibly standing for Thomas Conway. It is not believed that Catherine had been acting as a prostitute, even though she was known to drink. She had a number of possessions on her, from knick-knacks to clay pipes, and wore a silk around her neck. Her body appeared to have been posed after the murder. She was laid on her back, head towards the left shoulder, and arms laid to her sides with the palm upwards.

The Canonical Five

Similar to all of the victims associated with Jack the Ripper, her throat was slashed, cut clear to the vertebrae. However, her face had many different cuts, including deep into the bridge of her nose and part of her lip was removed. She was brutally mutilated and her face was just short of being unidentifiable.

Her death was believed to be caused by the cut to the throat, which severed the carotid artery, and the mutilation is believed to have occurred after the death; the body was mostly warm and fresh blood clots suggested she had barely been dead a half an hour when found. Her case is also perceived to have been done by an expert: the left kidney was completely taken out, intestines were placed about the body, the womb was mostly removed and stab wounds were found in the liver and the left groin.

It was believed that all of the wounds were consistent with those of a sharp blade approximately 6in long. The wounds were more random and there was much more mutilation than the previous murders associated with Ripper. Catherine Eddowes was not missing the same organs as Annie Chapman, and the stab wounds were not consistent with those of Polly Nichols, but she had been killed in the same way, with no signs of struggle and few bruises about the body.

Mary Jane Kelly

Mary Jane Kelly is the last victim accepted by the research of Sir Melville Macnaghten and the last of the five accepted as the Canonical Five by Ripperologists. Mary Jane Kelly was known by many aliases, including Mary Ann Kelly, which was also an alias used by other women, including Catherine Eddowes.

Her history is little known, and Joseph Barnett gave the only reports of her, with no substantial evidence to support any of it and much of it contradictory. The people who knew her said that she was well liked, and, unless she was drinking, was quiet and agreeable. Her history was believed to include time spent at a high-end brothel, and her background to be Welsh, though others thought it to be Irish.

The night leading up to her death had more sightings than any other of the Jack the Ripper murders. At 11pm she was seen drunk with a well-dressed young man, who had a moustache. Another person, Mary Ann Cox, saw Mary Jane walking with a stout man believed to be in his mid-30s, who was dressed quite shabbily and had side-whiskers and also a moustache.

Neighbours complained that she sang in her room at least until 1am, but at 2am, a George Hutchinson sees Kelly on Commercial Street, where she asks him for a sixpence. When he told her he had none she bid him a good morning and headed off. After this, it was reported that Kelly met a man that Hutchinson had just passed. The man carried a parcel and Kelly talked and laughed with him. Hutchinson later described seeing them outside the Queen's Head public house, where he noticed the man had pale skin, a moustache that turned up at the corners, dark hair and eyes and bushy eyebrows. It was 3am when Hutchinson left, having seen Kelly leave. However, it is not clear when she arrived home. She was reportedly seen by other people hours after her death, which was found to be confusing by police and the claims were ignored.

On 9th November, 1888, at 10:45am, Mary Jane Kelly, at the time identified as Marie Jeanette Kelly or Davies, was found mutilated inside her room at 26 Dorset Street, Spitalfields. Her description was that of a slim, blonde woman between the ages of 24 and 25 with a soft and attractive appearance. No neighbours reported any type of disturbance during the early morning hours after her singing earlier; however, a window was broken and blood was found on the glass.

Kelly's death was caused by the slash across her throat, although no signs of struggle were present. It was also noted that other than the broken glass there was no indication that anyone had forced their way into her room. The mutilation of her body was horrendous. Death was a direct result of blood loss from the cut across her throat. Her face was so mutilated that it was difficult to identify, pieces completely removed and slashes that drove deeply into her features. Her nose and ears were completely removed and strips of her flesh had been cut away from her skin to reveal the bone beneath. Her clothes had been neatly arranged and placed by the fireplace. The murderer had rested her body on the bed and carefully removed organs, placing them around her body, though some appeared to be missing all together.

As with the other murders, the cause of the damage was believed to be a sharp knife, some 6–8in long. Of all the murders, this one seemed to be the most involved: organs were moved about her body, and carefully arranged, but to what point no one was certain. The uterus, kidneys and a breast were found under her head, while her liver was between her feet and her other breast beside her right foot. Intestines were spread along her right side and the spleen was carefully placed outside her body to the left. Sections of her skin were even located next to the bed on the table.

Later the reports would include that her heart had been removed and was not found at the crime scene. Sections of her eyes and ears were completely removed, part of her lung had been torn away, her neck was cut clear through into the vertebrae, and even gashes and cuts were located in the legs and buttocks. The body was torn and cut away throughout and blood pooled under the bed. The crime ranks amongst the worst of the murders associated with Jack the Ripper.

Mary Ann Kelly was the last of the Canonical Five although over the years, it was suggested other deaths were down to Jack the Ripper, or a copycat killer.

Chapter 7

Modus Operandi

Modus Operandi

> The Ripper's signature revolved around his sexual violence. He is known to have taken complete control of his victims before, during and after he killed them. He also procured pleasure from the physical act of cutting, slicing and stabbing - penetrating the flesh of his victims. It's believed that this gruesome pleasure was in time elated to a sexual level.

The Latin phrase *modus operandi,* or M.O., translates to 'method of operation', which is an essential element of criminal profiling. Even in the case of the Ripper murders, the killer's signature and M.O. could help us in narrowing down what he was like and what could have motivated the killings. Being one of the biggest unsolved crimes in history, modern criminology continues to look through and discover more about the murders committed by Jack the Ripper. This chapter will give you an insight into how Jack killed his victims and whether or not he followed any killing rituals.

Victimology

Just like many other murder cases, studying the background and facts surrounding the victims can give us a better idea of why Jack the Ripper chose them. In any investigative process, victimology plays an essential role in understanding the relationship between the victim and the perpetrator. It also tells us whether or not the victims had any connections or similarities, which means that we can also find out why they were killed. This gets us closer to understanding the killer and solving the crime.

The killings possibly began on 31 August 1888 with Mary Ann Nichols – a forty-two year old prostitute and a mother of five, who had been separated from her husband for about nine years. She was approximately 157.5 cm tall and had brown or grey eyes. Her complexion was dark and her hair was dark brown with hints of greying. A known drinker, Nichols had been a workhouse inmate before. She was found lying on her back, dressed, but with her clothes pulled up to her stomach and her throat slashed from ear to ear.

During the early mornings of 8 September 1888, Annie Chapman suffered the same fate as Mary Ann Nichols. Chapman was a widow between forty-five and forty-seven years of age and was known to work as a prostitute. She was 152.4 cm tall and had a fair complexion with blue eyes and dark brown hair. Her physical appearance indicated she was malnourished and was possibly suffering from tuberculosis and syphilis. She was wearing old and dirty clothing, bearing the mark of Lambeth Workhouse. Like Nichols, Chapman was also found lying on her back with her throat cut from left to right, but in two places.

Next to suffer at the hands of the Ripper was a forty-five year old Swedish woman named Elizabeth Gustafsdotter Stride, also known as 'Long Liz'. She was a known prostitute and stood approximately 160 cm tall. She had a pale complexion and light grey eyes with dark, curly hair. Her body was found on 30 September 1888 at approximately 1 am. Both Stride and Chapman had handkerchiefs around their necks when they were found.

Around the same time on 30 September 1888, the body of Catherine Eddowes was found lying in a pool of blood. She was between the ages of forty-three and forty-six, about 152 cm tall, and had hazel eyes and auburn hair. Also known as Conway, Eddowes was not a prostitute at the time but she was known to be a heavy drinker. She sometimes cleaned homes or hawked on the streets to earn a living. On her left arm, she had a tattoo of the letters 'TC' in blue ink.

The mutilated body of Mary Jeanette Kelly, commonly called Mary Jane Kelly, was found on 9 November 1888. Now, with this case, the Ripper completely changed his victimology. Kelly was a well-known prostitute but unlike the others, she was blond and between the ages of 24 and 25. She was also taller than the previous victims, standing at 5½ft. She was also a heavy drinker but rarely drank to the extent of being helpless.

With the last victim, the Ripper also changed the location of his murders, possibly due to the increased police presence in the East End streets. It would have been very difficult for him to take his time in mutilating his victims with increased police scrutiny out of doors. While the previous killings occurred on the streets during the early morning hours, Mary Jane Kelly was brutally killed in bed inside an apartment building. In addition to being the youngest of Jack's victims, Kelly also suffered the most in terms of body mutilation, which we will discuss later on in this chapter.

The five women mentioned above have been considered as the confirmed victims of Jack the Ripper. However, there were several other murders bearing a close similarity to Jack's signature M.O. and victimology. Before Nichols, there was a possible Ripper victim named Emma Elizabeth Smith – a forty-five year old woman with light brown hair and a fair complexion. Like most of the other victims, Smith was about 5ft tall.

In the case of Emma Elizabeth Smith, the victim was able to return to the lodging house in which she was staying after being assaulted. According to the statements she made before her death, the brutal assault was made by three attackers, with the likely motive being robbery. The cause of death was determined as peritonitis, which was caused by the rupturing of the peritoneum.

Shortly before the murder of the first confirmed victim, the body of Martha Tabram was discovered lying on her back with her legs lying open and exposed. Tabram was about 36 years old and 5¼ft tall. She was well nourished and had a dark complexion with dark hair. Like the other victims, Tabram was also a heavy drinker and a prostitute. The main difference was the absence of throat slashing. Instead, this woman suffered approximately 39 stab wounds, mainly on the left side of her body. A stab to the heart was the cause of death for Tabram.

As we can see from the Canonical Five, the Ripper mainly chose high-risk victims – mostly prostitutes with drinking problems. None of them worked at brothels, but plied their trade in the dangerous and crime-ridden streets of Whitechapel. He primarily targeted women in their 40s, but for some reason switched to a younger victim in the last confirmed case. Expert profilers believe that Jack was at least partly motivated by a tortured sexual pathology. This would make it perfectly logical for him to target prostitutes representing sexuality and sex.

What is worthy of noting is that on 30 September 1888, there were two victims, both killed at around the same time at different locations. Double murders are not unheard of but quite uncommon, even for serial killers. The first victim of the night, Elizabeth Stride, was killed but not mutilated. It could indicate that Jack was interrupted, preventing him from getting the sexual gratification that he needed from mutilating his victim's body. He then moved to Catherine Eddowes and finally finished with his 'work' for the night.

Characteristics of the Ripper's Modus Operandi

According to the *Journal of Investigative Psychology and Offender Profiling,* the Canonical Five murders were committed by the same man. It is quite probable that he also murdered Martha Tabram. In these six cases, the *modus operandi* included attacks on white females between the ages of twenty-four and forty-five from the underclass society. The evidence suggests that the killer grabbed these women by the throat and brutally strangled them as they hiked their skirts up to prepare for sex.

He then lowered them to the ground, their heads normally pointing toward his left side – a conclusion made from the coroner's reports noting the lack of bruising on the head.

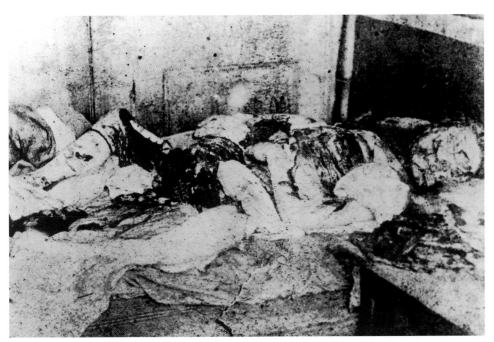

The mutilated body of Mary Jane Kelly, last victim of Jack the Ripper, as it was found in her squalid room at 13 Miller's Court in the East End of London, 9th November 1888.

A newspaper illustration showing the discovery of the mutilated body of Mary Jane Kelly, victim of Jack the Ripper, 9th November 1888.

A photograph of the outside of Mary Kelly's lodging house at 13 Miller's Court, taken the day after her murder. Through the broken window (arrowed), Thomas Bowyer made his horrific discovery, 9th November 1888.

x

An illustration depicting the police breaking open the door at 13 Miller's Court, Dorset Street, Spitalfields, where the body of Mary Jane Kelly had been seen through a broken window, 9th November 1888.

An illustration of Thomas Bowyer who, collecting rent, saw the body of Mary Jane Kelly through the broken window of the house at 13 Miller's Court, Dorset Street, Spitalfields, 9th November 1888.

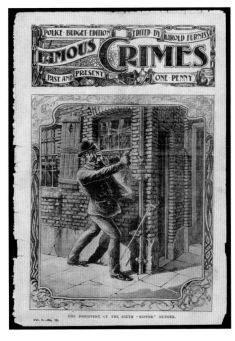

A view of Dorset Street, Spitalfields, in the East End of London. It is sometimes referred to as 'The Worst Street in London', and was the location of the murder of Mary Jane Kelly by Jack the Ripper, 1888.

A drawing of the body of Whitechapel prostitute, Alice Mackenzie who was found with her throat cut. Police suspected she may have been murdered by notorious killer Jack the Ripper, 17th July 1889.

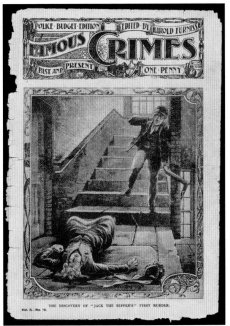

An illustration depicting John Saunders Reeves, a dock labourer, discovering the body of Martha Tabram on the landing at 37 George Yard Buildings, a possible first victim of Jack the Ripper, 7th August 1888.

A photograph of James Maybrick, a merchant, who was a suspect in the Jack the Ripper case, 1888.

An illustration depicting Mrs Florence Maybrick and the late James Maybrick. She was eventually imprisoned for poisoning him. 1889.

A photograph of Mrs Florence Maybrick who was imprisoned for poisoning her husband, James Maybrick, a suspect in the Jack the Ripper case, 1892.

A photograph of Albert Victor, Duke of Clarence and Avondale who was a suspect in the Whitechapel murder case, and who died of pneumonia aged 28, 1892.

He was mostly active during the darkest hours, making his abhorrent attacks between midnight and early mornings. In addition, he committed his crimes toward the end of the week. All six murders occurred within a three-month period and all six locations were within a one-mile square area.

The Ripper did not move the bodies of his victims after killing them. Before he cut their throats using a sharpened long knife, he would manually strangulate them till they were dead or unconscious. Instead of cutting their throats while standing, he cut them from the left after they fell to the ground. This conclusion was reached due to the coroner's reports and from the lack of bloodstains on their clothing. The throats of the victims were typically cut from left to right.

With Martha Tabram, he attacked her from the front and began a ghastly stabbing frenzy. This means that the killer would have been soaked in the blood of the victim, increasing the risk of being discovered. From the (possibly) first killing, the killer learned quickly and soon adapted his *modus operandi*. He began carrying out his attacks from behind instead of from the front of his victims, slashing their throats and incapacitating them. This would also result in minimal blood spatter and stains on his own clothing, decreasing the chances of being discovered on his way home.

This change in M.O. was apparent in all the cases of the

Canonical Five. Most of his attacks were made outdoors. However, the killer was not hesitant to change the location of his murders when the opportunity presented itself. In the case of Kelly, he carried out a far more brutal and time-consuming act behind closed doors. Some experts claim that this change in the murder location cannot be considered as a change in the killer's characteristic pattern but more like a natural progression of his needs.

According to the coroner's reports from the murder of Martha Tabram, nine out of the 39 stab wounds could be found on her throat. Seventeen of the stabs were inflicted on her breasts and a few more on the lower parts of the body. The time of her death was somewhere between 2:00 and 4:50 am. From the reports, we also know that the lungs were severely damaged – the left one having been penetrated in five places and the right one in two. A one-time penetration to the heart was determined as the cause of death.

There were five places of penetration in the liver, as well, two in the spleen and six in the stomach. The neck and genitals also suffered a few wounds and the doctors even identified a wound that seemed to penetrate the chest bone. It was concluded that the wounds were not inflicted by the same instrument but were also consistent with penetration by a sharp instrument like a dagger or a knife. Every wound was inflicted before the victim died.

When Mary Ann Nichols' body was found, it was still warm and the wound inflicted on her throat was still oozing blood. Her clothes were disarranged, despite the fact that she was still clothed. The backside of her coat was soaked in blood and her bonnet was lying by the right side of the body. It was obvious that the killer had left her body exposed in the open, so she could be quickly discovered. The absence of drag marks nearby and the blood pool under the body suggest that he left her on the same spot as the murder.

Upon examination, it was determined that the killer had cut through the spinal cord and the windpipe gullet. In fact, he had cut her throat so deeply that he nearly severed her head from her body. With the incisions going as long as 8in, the killer may have been using a sharp, long-bladed knife. Bruises were found on her left cheek and her lower right jaw, consistent with bruising caused by a fist or a thumb or even fingers. There was a slight laceration found on the tongue and five teeth were missing from her mouth. The absence of bruising on the arms indicates that there was no kind of struggle.

There was a jagged cut along her abdomen, with several cuts on the coating of the stomach. Doctors also identified two stab wounds on the genitalia. It was concluded that the abdominal injuries were the first to be inflicted, causing instantaneous death. However, blood evidence also suggests that the neck wounds occurred before Nichols received the abdominal injuries. In addition, the killer inflicted many of the injuries while the victim was on the ground.

Annie Chapman was missing two of her lower teeth when her dead body was found lying on her back. The neck of her jacket had bloodstains on the inside and her left sleeve was also stained with a few droplets of blood. These suggest that the victim had suffered a neck injury, which resulted in this blood spatter pattern. A few blood spatters could also be found on her stockings, which could have come from the abdominal injuries she received while on the ground. Police did not find any evidence of a struggle or any weapons on the scene.

Bruises could be found on the upper eyelid and over the right temple along with two distinct bruise marks on the front of her chest. Each bruise appeared to be about the size of a man's thumb. Her face was swollen and turned toward the right, and her tongue had protruded out of her teeth, but not outside the mouth. She was found with her legs drawn up and her left arm resting on her left breast. She appeared as if she had been reaching for her throat, as both hands were raised and bent with her palms facing toward the upper body. Her right hand had a bruise in the middle.

Chapman's small intestines were missing, while the rest of the intestines were intact. The flap of the abdomen was placed above the right shoulder and it was still attached to her body by a cord. Above the left shoulder in a pool of blood, there were two other flaps of skin taken from the lower part of the abdomen. There was a deep and jagged cut around the throat, which appeared to have started from the left. Evidence suggests that the killer had seized the victim by the throat while making the cuts. Upon closer examination, it was discovered that there were abrasion marks and distinct ring markings on the ring finger. This indicated that the killer had forcibly removed whatever rings the victim had been wearing.

There were several body parts missing from Chapman's body, including the womb, the navel and some other parts of the belly wall, and the upper portion of the vagina. She was also missing a huge portion of the bladder. The coroner believed that the killer had some knowledge of the human anatomy from the way he had removed the viscera. The cuts suggest that the weapon used was thin and narrow with a sharp blade, which was about 6–8in in length. Instead of using a regular knife, the killer might have used either an amputating knife or a slaughter man's knife.

From available physical evidence, experts believe that the victim had been seized by the chin from behind, with her throat pressed hard. This would have resulted in suffocation and unconsciousness. There was no sign of sexual assault or a struggle. The killer had unnecessarily inflicted injury to the viscera, while loss of blood from the neck injury was sufficient to result in death. He was careful to empty the contents of her pockets and then arrange them in order at her feet. However, the forcible removal of the rings suggests that he might have been interrupted.

Like with Mary Ann Nichols, Elizabeth Stride's body was still warm when it was discovered lying on her left side with her legs drawn up. The silk handkerchief around her throat had a small tear that corresponded to the angle of her right jaw. In addition to the deep gash on her throat, she also had a skin abrasion below her right brow. Her front upper teeth were missing. Her right hand lay open on her chest, smeared in blood both inside and out. There was a long incision in the neck, beginning from the left side and severing the vessels located about 1½in from the jaw line.

There was no sign of blood on any of the clothing. Her dress had been undone at the top. Evidence indicated that the victim bled out slowly and was unable to call out for help because of her severed windpipe. It's possible that the killer was able to grab a hold of the victim's scarf to pull her backward. However, there is no sufficient evidence to determine whether or not the victim had been standing when the killer cut her throat.

In the case of Catherine Eddowes, her skirt had been pulled up over her waist when she was found. The upper part of her body, including her head, neck, and shoulders were drenched in the blood pool. She had been wearing an apron, a part of which had been cut through, and then found inside her dress. Another portion of her apron was found on Gouldstone Street, where the nearby wall had a chalk writing of the words 'The Juwes are the men That Will not be Blamed for nothing'.

It appeared as if her body had been posed, so that she was lying on her back and her head was turned to her left. Both arms were by her side with her palms upward, a thimble lying next to her fingers on the right side. The killer had enough time to draw her skirt up over her abdomen and expose her naked thighs. Her face was immensely disfigured and her throat cut, a neckerchief tied just below the cut. Like Annie Chapman, Eddowes was also severely and horribly mutilated. Her intestines were lying over her right shoulder with fecal matter smeared over them.

A piece of intestine was found between her left arm and her body. Her right ear had been cut so deeply that the lobe and auricle were cut through obliquely. While her body was still warm, the blood on the pavement had clotted. This indicated that she could have been dead for about half an hour when she was found. According to the autopsy record, Eddowes was missing her uterus and her left kidney. However, there was no evidence to suggest that the mutilation was carried out by someone with anatomical skills.

The renal artery on the left was severed and so was the left carotid artery, which was determined as the cause of death.

A portion of her lip and the tip of her nose had also been cut off, with several cuts on the face and one deep cut in the bridge of her nose. Doctors were able to identify a few stab wounds – one stab to the liver and one to the left groin. Although the cervix and vagina remained intact, a large portion of the womb had been removed. The weapon used was determined as a sharp knife of about 6in in length.

Mary Jane Kelly's body was found stretched out on the bed and severely mutilated. Like Eddowes, her ears and nose had been cut off. Her eyebrows and cheeks were also partially removed and her face was gashed in different directions. Despite the disembowelment and body mutilation, the scene had comparatively little blood. The killer had removed the surface of her thighs and abdomen as well as the viscera from the abdominal cavity.

Under her head, some of the body parts, including one breast, the uterus, and the kidney were found. The other breast was lying by her right side and the spleen by her left. The mutilation was so severe that her neck was severed to the bone and her face was beyond recognition. Upon closer examination, it was discovered that the killer had opened the victim's pericardium and removed her heart, which could not be found at the scene of the crime.

The killer had made circular incisions to remove the victim's breasts and also removed the abdominal skin and tissues in large flaps. There were extensive jagged wounds on the arms and forearms of the victim, with a superficial incision in the right thumb. While the left lung remained in place, the lower part of the right lung had been broken and torn away. A few of the mutilations were performed after the victim succumbed to her injuries. Severing of the right carotid artery resulted in severe blood loss, which was determined as the cause of death.

Signature

Crime investigations cannot be complete with a thorough analysis of the perpetrator's signature characteristics. This is different from the M.O. because while M.O. points to the actions of the offender when carrying out and completing the crime, signature refers to the actions considered as unique to the offender and going beyond what is necessary to commit the crime. The *modus operandi* may change over time and reveal the nature of the crime, whereas the signature tends to remain the same and reveal the nature of the offender.

From the brutal cuts and injuries the killer inflicted upon his victims, we can see that his signature revolved around sexual violence. He is known to take control of his victims before, during, and after he killed them. His signature includes progressive picquerism, which refers to the development of his ability to derive sexual pleasure from cutting, slicing, or stabbing another person. Picquerism could also refer to the act of deriving sexual pleasure by observing these actions.

Primary mechanisms can give sexual satisfaction to some serial killers, but others need violence-related secondary mechanisms for the same kind of satisfaction. Experts believe that the Ripper made use of the violence of slashing or even stabbing his victims with a knife to exert his dominance and control over the women he attacked. Penetrating his victims with a knife could give him sexual stimulation. He could sexually satisfy himself from the domination of his victims as well as their mutilation and bleeding, instead of sexual intercourse.

Although not every Ripper victim received similar numbers or types of injuries, it was apparent that picquerism was a constant part of his signature. He progressed across a series of escalating levels of violence – from stabbing the genitalia and breasts of Martha Tabram to mutilating those parts in Mary Ann Nichols. He then moved on to harvesting the organs of Annie Chapman and Mary Jane Kelly. Signs of sexual activity or intercourse could not be found in any of the cases, but the sexual component of picquerism was obvious in all of them.

All six cases demonstrated the Ripper's need to fully incapacitate his victims for their immediate submission. From his attacks, we can see that he needed to immediately subdue and silence them before continuing with more brutal acts of violence. Overkill was also a part of his signature, indicating his need to gain complete control and dominance over his victims. He inflicted fatal wounds in excessive numbers even beyond what was necessary for the victims to die.

He went on to bring further degradation to the victims by leaving their bodies in the open, where they could easily be discovered. It appeared as if he was 'flaunting' the dead bodies of his victims, probably considering himself as an invincible man. This also suggests that be believed himself to be in control and out of reach of both the public and the police.

Another apparent characteristic of Jack the Ripper's signature was the way he posed the dead bodies of his victims. Aside from the Stride case in which he was interrupted, every other victim was lying flat on her back with her legs spread. He carefully posed them in a sexually degrading manner with their genitals exposed. It is possible that this choice of position was to emphasize that these women were disposable.

As his signature gradually evolved, he began to remove the organs and arrange them in a specific manner. He typically left the viscera at the scene, but outside of the body. It is believed that this mutilation could be an attempt to rob the victims of their humanity as well as to horrify and shock whoever found the bodies. Mutilation was a consistent element in all cases except for the murder of Elizabeth Stride – the interruption meant he wouldn't have had the time to mutilate her body.

Every case showed evidence of the extensive planning the killer might have put into the attacks. This is clear from the fact that the killer carried his weapon with him and also took it with him after the murders. In addition, some planning and experience would have been necessary to leave no signs of struggle with his victims. With many of the other killings that were presumed but not confirmed to be the works of the Ripper, experts were unable to detect any escalating pattern in the signature behaviours of the killer, or killers.

Profile

According to a profile made by Roy Hazelwood and John Douglas in the book *The Cases That Haunt Us,* Jack the Ripper might have been a paranoid and disorganized killer. They believed he was a white male in his late twenties or early thirties. It was likely that he grew up in a household dominated by a woman who may have been either promiscuous or taken to drinking. This means that his early childhood years were marked by the absence and, or passiveness of his father.

Hazelwood and Douglas also believed that he was an introvert and an antisocial loner who expressed his anger by torturing animals and setting fires. By the time he committed the murders, he had become inconspicuous, calm, and quiet. If he was employed, it was likely in a profession that allowed him to pursue his interests, such as a butcher or a morgue worker. It is also possible that he worked as a low-ranking hospital staff or even a mortician's assistant, judging by the fact that he had some knowledge of the human anatomy.

From the time of the murders, we can assume that his job gave him days off on certain holidays and weekends. He was probably single and living alone, so that he could come home and leave as he pleased without raising suspicion. In addition, it was likely that Jack the Ripper came from a poor household and was from the same socio-economic class as the victims. He probably lived in the area because he was able to move around in blood-spattered clothing (from the Tabram murder) without anyone noticing.

Before the murders, it is possible that he visited the pubs in the Whitechapel area to drown his sorrows and tensions in drink. Since all his victims were heavy drinkers, he may have been acquainted with them at least once in these pubs. It is believed that he was nocturnal and may have prowled the streets of the neighbourhood in search of potential victims. Some even believe that the police may have interrogated him about the murders at some point.

Some experts say that the Ripper might have been suffering from a poor self-image and even had a physical disability or disfigurement. He may have felt inadequate as a social outcast, only contributing to his pent-up desire for violence. This negative self-image would have accounted for the paranoid traits of the killer. He might have even carried one or more knives to defend himself. It is likely that he did not have the courage to express his violence in everyday life, choosing to take it out on his victims to a grotesque extent.

Growing up in a household controlled by a dominating mother might have resulted in his hatred for women. At the same time, he was also fearful of the opposite sex, but most would not consider him as a viable suspect because of his quiet and innocuous nature. It is difficult to believe that these were his first attacks against women. He may have been less violent in the previous incidents, meaning the earlier attacks would have gone unreported or were not investigated thoroughly. This is especially likely if the complaints came from prostitutes.

According to Douglas, the Ripper could be classified as an opportunistic killer rather than a preferential killer. He chose prostitutes with drinking problems because they were easy targets. He was a lust killer, which means that his ritual mutilations were focused on the female genitalia. However, the murders were not necessarily sexual in nature because there was no evidence to suggest that he had sexual intercourse with his victims before or after killing them. Instead, the mutilations indicate that he could be acting out violent fantasies targeting his dominant mother. Douglas believes that Jack's mother was the source of the image he had of women. He probably despised her and women in general because of her drinking problem, or promiscuous nature.

Most of the Ripper profiles made by different experts have been uniform with a few variations. In the original profile created by Dr Thomas Bond in 1889, he mentioned that the attacks were clearly motivated by the killer's sexual needs. He also believed that the killer was quiet but had an inoffensive appearance with a mental problem, and probably even suffered from a type of sexual deviancy known as Satyriasis.

From these notes, we can see a clear distinction between the M.O. and the signature of Jack the Ripper. In the six cases, his M.O. evolved with experience, as he began to discover what he liked and did not like. For instance, the killer wanted to minimize the chances of detection and interruption in the case of Mary Jane Kelly. Committing the murder indoors gave him more time to do what he pleased, even after the victim succumbed to her injuries.

In regards to his signature, the key characteristics remained the same and from the available evidence, experts were able to determine that all six murders were committed by the same person. Signature analysis failed to link the other murders to the cases of the Canonical Five and that of the Martha Tabram murder. Some of the later Whitechapel murders will be discussed in the next chapter. The mystery surrounding Jack the Ripper may never be solved, but modern investigative techniques have helped us get a clearer picture of what the killer was like and why he killed.

Chapter 8

Other Whitechapel Murders

Other
Whitechapel Murders

In addition to the possibly invented victims, it is possible that early murders attributed to other violent happenings were actually the early attempts of Jack the Ripper. In many studies, serial killers have demonstrated a tendency towards prior incidents before their first successful kills. While some killers may begin by killing or torturing small animals, others may simply have failed attempts prior to their first successful kill.

In 1888, Whitechapel saw some of the highest murder statistics ever recorded, even though not all the Ripper cases occurred that year. While researchers disagree which of the killings were genuinely Ripper crimes, the sensationalism perpetrated by the newspapers of the day firmly put the spotlight on Jack. In the mid-1900s, investigations were reopened again on the cold cases around the time of the Whitechapel murders.

However, the trail had been muddied at certain stages by writers who invented murdered women; such is the case with Fairy Fay who reportedly died a vicious death in December of

1887. However, the two authors responsible were not able to provide any source of evidence. There is no evidence of any such murder having occurred nor are there any death records bearing the same name. While the vision of an even earlier attack possibly occurring is on the mind of every researcher, this particular victim left no paperwork or evidence of existence.

The Attacks of 1888

Many behaviourists and criminal investigators reason that most serial killers do not begin their crime spree successfully or directly with murders. It is likely that they first have unsuccessful attempts at murder or successful attempts at violence that end in the victim's death. Unlike the other Whitechapel attacks, these incidents resulted in the women fighting back and the culprit escaping.

Annie Millwood was attacked and stabbed on 25th February 1888. She was not killed instantly, but died weeks later. Her case has been attributed to the Whitechapel murders owing to the similarities between herself and Martha Tabram, both in ages (barely a year difference), location of the incident – Tabram was killed just a short distance away at George Yard – and the stabbing wounds found on the body.

Similarly to Millwood, an unknown assailant attacked and also stabbed Ada Wilson on 28th March 1888, at 2:30am at her home in Mile End. However, unlike other suspected Ripper accounts, this particular incident included a demand for money after the man forced his way into her house. Wilson survived two stabs to the throat.

Another similar event to the previous two included a man who supposedly attempted to cut the throat of Annie Farmer on the morning of 21st November 1888. The wound on her neck was not deep and though she never recanted her story, she did not provide enough evidence to capture her assailant. The attacker was a man she had brought home with her, and described as having a dark complexion, dark hair with moustache, a suit and a black felt hat. He was around 36 years old and 5ft 6in tall.

Although it is likely she intended to have sex with the man, it is believed she might have tried to rob him because coins were discovered in her mouth. She cut herself when the situation did not go as planned and the man likely ran away rather than defend himself from fear of a possible lynch mob. As the wound was only mild, it is believed that the sharp knife, thought to have been the chosen weapon of the Ripper, could not have caused it.

Mysterious Bodies

During the Whitechapel murders, body parts were discovered in the Thames. This became of great concern because the victims could not be identified. It seemed that either Jack the Ripper had a split personality, or had competition for who was to commit the most brutal murder – the victims were even more mutilated than those of the Canonical Five.

They were cut and wrapped in clothes and tied with bootlaces, and their heads were missing. The murders were considered closely related to the Ripper crimes, even to the point of suggesting the same person killed them. However, many distinct differences existed between the method of death. This murderer would come to be referred to as the Torso Killer The torso of a woman was found on 3rd October 1888 on the site where Scotland Yard police HQ was being built in central London and the case became known as the Whitehall Mystery.

It was revealed that the woman was probably in her early 20s, having had no children and had been dead for as long as two months before being dumped in a cellar. Later, other dismembered remains of the same woman, including an arm, were found in two other locations. However, the body could not be linked to any missing women. The torso had no wounds, only jagged cuts and there was speculation that the murderer had experience in wrapping, as the body had been quite deftly covered. It was thought that the murderer behind a similar crime, the Pinchin Street torso, was responsible.

During the early weeks of June, in 1889, more body parts were found in the Thames. Most pieces were wrapped up in strange packages tied in bootlaces. They came in sections along the river and it was discovered that the victim had been at least seven months pregnant and was between 20–30 years old. The child of the woman had been removed after her death.

Later, it became known that an Elizabeth Jackson, who was pregnant, had gone missing in late May. By identification of a scar on her wrist, she was identified as the victim. The search and investigation did not recover her heart or her head. It is believed she may have been working as a prostitute. Unlike the Ripper murders, this crime was recognized as the work of a butcher and perceived to be the same culprit behind the Whitehall Mystery and the Pinchin torso.

The Pinchin Street torso (The Torso), was recognised as the tenth Whitechapel Murder victim and she was believed to have been murdered on 8th September 1889. The torso was discovered under a railway arch at 5:15am on 10th September 1889, by PC William Pennett. The arms were later discovered nearby, and some bloodstained clothing was located on Batty

Street. The body was estimated to be that of a 30-to-40-year-old female. Some researchers attributed the crime to the Ripper as the body had similar mutilation as his victims, and it came on the one-year anniversary of one of his killings. However, it is likely that while these particular murders can be associated with each other, they are not the work of Jack the Ripper owing to the differences in styles. This suggests that during this time period there were possibly two active serial killers in the region, with this particular killer attacking younger women.

Other Murders in 1888 and 1889

A number of murders were committed between 1888 and 1889, and of these, only five were associated with Jack the Ripper, three were attributed to the Torso Killer, and the rest were referred to as having been committed by person or persons unknown. Many researchers have commented on the large number of enquiries ending in the decision of "murder by person or persons unknown", however, it is essential to remember that this was a time prior to fingerprinting, widespread surveillance equipment and DNA testing.

These murders were committed in a time when conclusions were garnered by the people finding the body and the doctors who examined the corpse. Little could be done to ascertain even who had been into a room prior to the victim's death. Investigations relied heavily on individual accounts by eyewitnesses or parties of interest. Short of a confession or a witness, finding the murderers would have been difficult.

Emma Smith died on the 3rd April 1888, from a coma that was brought on by being brutally assaulted on Osborn Street. Emma was a prostitute known for being able to defend herself and she had even managed to get help after the attack. Emma was able to identify her assailants as being three men. In addition, she was robbed, brutally beaten and raped.

While listed in the crimes possibly committed by Jack the Ripper, the connection is unlikely owing to it being so much different from all the other recognised victims and being inconsistent with the theory that the Ripper was a single individual.

Martha Tabram was killed on the 7th August 1888. Many witnesses knew her as a perpetual alcoholic whose every last shilling went on drink. On the very night of her murder, she had wandered off from her friend Mary Ann Connolly – aka Pearly Polly – to have sex with a guardsman. Her body was discovered later in the George Yard Buildings at 4:45am. She had at least 22 knife wounds spread about the torso, with multiple other wounds in the legs and throat, possibly created by a penknife. One larger wound found on her body was in the sternum and may have been caused by a dagger or bayonet. Her murder was unlike the murders most often associated with the Ripper and possibly included rape owing to the way she was killed and the position in which her body was found.

Rose Mylett's death on 20th December 1888 was the most complicated of the deaths reported during this time, as a number of doctors were called in to review the body. While most thought her death was caused by strangulation, one doctor, Thomas Bond of Westminster, diagnosed the death accidental and self-inflicted owing to suffocation on vomit, caused by the tightness of the collar on the outfit she had been wearing.

Mylett's body was found in Clarke's Yard, Poplar High Street, where she was reportedly lying on the ground with no signs of struggle or evidence that any other person had been within the vicinity. Eyewitness reports said she had been drinking, but no alcohol was found in her system. To complicate things further, she appeared to have different names in many different places. Family explanations and tales of her history were unverifiable and to date no one is quite sure exactly who this woman was. No evidence of her having given birth in years was found during the post mortem, yet Mylett's mother reported that she was estranged from her husband and had a child who would be aged seven, named Florrie or Flossie. No supporting evidence was ever found to confirm any of the conflicting information and few authors connected her to the Ripper murders.

A rarely mentioned murder victim was a seven-year old boy named John Gill. The boy was found in Manningham, Bradford, with severe mutilations, including his abdomen being sliced open and his intestines pulled out. The boy's legs had been severed and his heart along with an ear was removed. His murder resulted in the arrest of his employer, William Barrett, twice, however, no substantial evidence could be found to implicate the man in the boy's murder. John is often eliminated from the list of possible Ripper victims owing to his gender, age and the differences in his mutilation.

Alice McKenzie was one of the least known victims in Whitechapel between 1888 and 1889. She was believed to have engaged in prostitution when her death occurred. However, her past is much of a mystery, including the date of her birth. Her body was found in Castle Alley by PC Walter Andrews on 17th July 1889. Similarly to the Ripper victims, she had been attacked with a knife, though it may have been a small one. None of the cuts had been driven deep into her body and the markings suggested a left-handed rather than a right-handed man. The cuts into her throat were stabs rather than the deep slash that was clearly present in the Ripper murders and the mutilation of her torso was shallow according to the post mortem.

Later Similar Murders

While it is conventionally considered that the final murder representing the work of Jack the Ripper occurred with Kelly in November of 1888, other killings have been associated with him. Some authors have even suggested that he later moved on to other areas, such as the Americas, and was the perpetrator of a horrific string of murders that later occurred in South America. In addition, these three particular cases are often highlighted in the history.

Person or persons unknown murdered Frances Coles in the very early hours of 13th February 1891, at age 31. Ernest Thompson, who heard the receding footsteps of who he believed to be the murderer, discovered her nearly dead body in Swallow Gardens on Chamber Street, but as Frances was still alive and bleeding, he could not leave her. Also known as Frances Coleman, Francis Hawkins and Carroty Nell, Frances was the daughter of a bootmaker and had not told her family her profession, though it is believed she had been a prostitute for as many as eight years. She had been forced to the ground where the attacker made three attempts with a blunt knife to cut open her throat.

The prime suspect was a James Sadler who had previously been both a seaman and a firefighter. During the night before Frances's murder, she had spent time with Sadler and had argued with him. Much of the night and morning around

Frances's death, Sadler had spent engaging in drunken brawls and trying to convince lodging houses to grant him a place to sleep. This murder was not associated to Sadler nor the Ripper.

Carrie Brown, also known as Old Shakespeare, was killed on 24th April 1891, in the rented room of the East River Hotel on the Manhattan waterfront of New York. While many differences exist between the crimes of Whitechapel and this one, Brown was also a prostitute, possibly 56-years old. She had been with a man when renting the hotel room and her murderer attempted to mutilate the body in much the same way as the Ripper.

Much of this particular story was not verifiable short of the death certificate, and her history, even her birthday is lost. Her death was similar to the Whitechapel murders and she too suffered mutilation with her ovary cut out. It has been suggested that it may have been an attempt to imitate the horrific murders of Whitechapel. However, it is unlikely that this was a Ripper murder and the NYPD refused to make a connection to the villain. An Algerian by the name of Ben Ali was tried and convicted. However, Ali was released from prison 11 years later following new information. The only other suspect was a young man from a nearby city who had long disappeared.

A more recent addition to the suspected Ripper murders is Emily Dimmock, who was found dead on 12th September

1907 at 29 St Paul's Road, Camden Town. This murder is commonly referred to as the Camden Town Murder and a man called Robert Wood, was tried and found not guilty. This particular case bears resemblance to Jack the Ripper as Emily was killed by a sharp knife brought across her neck, which almost removed her head from her body. Though Emily Dimmock was in a long-term relationship with Bert Shaw, she was working as a prostitute in the late nights while Bert was working at the Midland Railway.

While three aspects of her death were similar to the Ripper murders, the third being that she apparently put up no resistance, it is unlikely this murder was truly a murder to be added to the Canonical Five because no mutilation had occurred to the torso and no organs were missing from the body. Later, authors would try to attribute this murder to Walter Sickert, another member on the suspect list for Jack the Ripper, however, nothing more than circumstantial and loose assumptions tie him to her murder.

All but this last victim have something in common; they were killed during the time of the Jack the Ripper and their murders remain unsolved. These women were mostly all streetwalkers and while this is not the first time in history prostitutes would be murdered en masse, it was the first set of killings believed to be the act of a serial killer. Since then Peter Sutcliffe (1975–1980), Gary Ridgway (1982–1998), Robert

Hansen (1980–1983), Joel Rifkin (1989–1993), have all been found guilty of similar crimes.

In each of the murders, even in the case where suspects were identified, no one was brought to justice. They are recognised as cold cases and intrigue the mystery-solvers of today. Through careful evaluation of the victims, a pattern could be discerned that may one day lead to the killer, however, the first step is to create a map of occurrences. To create this map it is essential to identify which of these murders were actually the work of Jack the Ripper and to determine if he engaged in unsuccessful attempts to murder prior to his success. Is it possible that he only killed his victims if they were resting or otherwise unsuspecting? Did he kill the boy that was found mutilated?

If each of these victims can be carefully placed into a map defining the activities of Jack the Ripper, it could be possible to identify where the Ripper came from or what might have been his activities prior to each murder. Could it be that he was simply wandering through Whitechapel? Might he have been a local resident who already knew each of these victims? These are the questions we have the luxury of asking today. It was so different in the 1880s when the people of East London were terrified of the beast roaming the dark streets and all they wanted was justice and protection.

Chapter 9

Scotland Yard

Scotland Yard

Known as 'The Weasel', Frederick Porter Wensley was one of the most promising detectives in Scotland Yard. He had joined the police as a young man in 1888 and his career was marked by a number of groundbreaking cases. One of the initial cases, the 'Blodie Belgium' case, was delegated to Wensley. The torso of a French woman, Emilienne Gerard, was found on the streets of London. A note saying 'Blodie Belgium' was found with it. In an ingenious investigative method, Wensley asked the woman's lover, Louis Voisin to write 'bloody Belgium' in his own hand. He made the same spelling mistake that was glaringly evident in the note and was arrestedt.

London in the 19th century was swiftly changing to become what would be the biggest city in the world. But rapid industrialisation was dividing the population into two distinct categories – the rich and the poor – and this demarcation was clearly seen in the areas they lived. England may have established its imperialist supremacy in the world, but the situation at home was far from ideal. The industrial revolution had left those that had work with a sense of unrest while those without jobs were becoming embittered.

The Need for New Police

London as a city was growing with the addition of places such as Paddington, Belgravia, Finsbury, Islington, Southwark, Lambeth, Holborn and Shoreditch in its territory. The city had emerged as the political, economic and trading centre of an all-powerful empire and quickly became the most popular destination for immigrants searching for a better life.

The policing system until the 19th century consisted of parish constables who were elected and appointed by the local authorities. It was voluntary and unpaid work, which did not have the slightest chance of being effective in the dark, secretive and ugly underbelly of a great city. The London Metropolitan police was established in 1829 under the guidance and charge of the then Home Minister, Robert Peel, through the Metropolitan Police Act. This police force came to be popularly known as 'bobbies' or 'peelers', an informal reference to the man behind the set-up. Robert Peel, as Home Secretary, appointed a committee to evaluate the policing system prevalent in those times.

According to the findings, given the backdrop of Victorian London, there was a need for a more organised and effective policing structure that needed to phase out the involvement of the military in the internal affairs of the country. Sir Robert, who later became the Prime Minister, expressed his ideas about the standardisation of the police force to parliament. He said policing should be looked on as a profession that pays, was close to the concerns of the general public and answerable to them as well. This new proposal found quick sanction by the Parliament and a law was passed in 1829 to set up a police force.

The Metropolitan Police Service, or the Met, as it was soon referred to, would be accountable directly to the Home Office with no participation of the local authorities. Peel said that crime would be controlled only when criminals felt with certainty that they would be caught, as compared to the degree of punishment dealt out for their crimes.

The main idea was to prevent crimes and the new force did not have any investigative authority whatsoever. They were not allowed to look into the personal lives of people and worked primarily as whistleblowers. People who had served in the army and had retired were considered for important positions to man the new force. Care was taken to make sure that these men had clean records and good reputations. Peel made the conscious effort to recruit reliable and hardworking people who knew London well and how things worked in the nooks and corners of the sprawling city.

The first two commissioners of the Met were Lieutenant Colonel Rowan and Sir Richard Mayne. Rowan was a retired army soldier while Mayne was a lawyer. The commissioner took the highest position in the organization and pains were taken to hire staff to work under these two men. There were approximately 1,000 men working for the Met from the beginning, including superintendents, inspectors, sergeants and constables. Despite initial friction, people soon started to rely on this new force.

Peel's Principles

Sir Robert Peel was very particular about the functions, rights, powers and duties of the Met. He set out nine principles that became the foundation of the new police. These principles in essence were:

- The primary function of the police is the prevention of both crime and disorder.

- The actions taken by the police are entirely dependent on approval by the people and their acceptance.

- The maintenance of the rights and dignity of citizens is of utmost importance and the police are to garner voluntary assistance from the people in the maintenance of law and order.

- The use of physical force by the police will not help in getting cooperation. In fact, it will achieve the opposite.

- The police will earn the favour of the people by being a

completely impartial force, rather than pandering to popular opinions.

- Only when polite verbal communication with people fails to achieve the desired results of law and order should the police revert to the use of physical violence.

- In essence, the police and the public are the same. The former is just a paid extension of the latter to completely focus on securing the welfare of their kind.

- All actions taken by the police need to be focused on doing their prescribed duties without threatening the judiciary and its powers in any way.

- The real test for the police is not the method in which results achieved but the results themselves, which is the absence of crime and instability in the society.

The Name of Scotland Yard

The headquarters of the Metropolitan Police was located in the Whitehall district of London. This district had some of the most important government offices, including the Ministry of Defence, the British Army and the Royal Navy. The building where this new police unit was set up had an enclosed yard called Great Scotland Yard nearby that led to an entrance for the public. It is since then and to date that this association lives, despite the move of the headquarters to Victoria Embankment in an ornate Italian-inspired brick building in 1890.

Metropolis Divisions

The Metropolitan Police Service was made responsible for preventing crime, managing crowds and the general upkeep of law and order in 17 divisions of the London metropolis that were being divided from 1829–1830. These divisions excluded the area of the City of London, which was the sole responsibility of a separate police force. Each division was denoted by a letter and had a separate police station. The letters from A–V denoted London boroughs:

A – Westminster
B – Chelsea
C – Mayfair, Soho
D – Marylebone
E – Holborn
F – Kensington
G – King's Cross
H – Stepney
K – West Ham
L – Lambeth
M – Southwark

N – Islington

P – Peckham

R – Greenwich

S – Hampstead

T – Hammersmith

V – Wandsworth

Later, in the years 1865 and 1866, four more divisions of W – Clapham, X – Willesden, Y – Tottenham and J – Bethnal Green were added to areas under the Met. People's reaction to the Metropolitan Police Service

The people of London did not react in a positive manner to the establishment of the police force. Some saw the police personnel as being natural allies to the military and did not want their presence to interfere in their day-to-day lives. They also believed that these people were in reality spies deployed by the government to keep an eye on people, especially those living in the East End.

Derogatory terms like Raw Lobsters, Peel's Bloody Gang and Blue Devils were hurled at the police in an attempt to undermine the authority they had over the people. Sir Robert Peel was an astute and practical politician and decided that the Metropolitan Police would have a different set of principles, to the military. To convince the people on the psychological level, he decided that the uniform of the police would be blue instead of red, which was the colour of the British military and induced fear among civilians. Policemen were not allowed to carry any weapons bar a truncheon made of wood and a rattle as an alarm.

Within the structural organisation of the force, only the military title of sergeant was to be used to denote one of the ranks. Peel also made sure that policemen were not allowed to carry guns on a regular basis, although the Commissioner was authorised to purchase over 50 pocket pistols, they were to be used only in the most extraordinary cases. In those days of extreme poverty and hunger, burglaries were the most common cases of crimes committed by thieves armed with guns.

During this period, only civilians who were Protestants in Christian England were allowed to carry any sort of firearm. After police fatalities to armed thieves, the Commissioner was forced to talk to Peel about removing the limitation on weapons carried by policemen. The request was granted with the condition that the issued revolvers would be handed over only to those officers deemed responsible enough. Eventually, newer systems would supplant these limitations and Scotland Yard continued to establish itself as a force to reckon with, not only in terms of weaponry, but also the might of its intelligence.

Public Order

The political atmosphere in Victorian England was not as intense as revolutionary Europe at that time but politicians were anxious to stifle any domestic unrest. The government actively discouraged people from gathering in large numbers in public places. It was also one of the main objectives of the Metropolitan Police Service to make sure that there was adherence to civilised and non-violent behaviour at such gatherings.

The period between 1839 and 1848 was marked by Chartist protests led by the working-class population who wanted political reform. The Met was successful in performing their duties throughout this phase. But on 13th November 1887, came what was known as Bloody Sunday. A demonstration was called by the Metropolitan Radical Federation and the Irish National League to protest against repression in Ireland, the imprisonment of Irish MPs and to assert the right to free speech.

Public meetings had been banned from Trafalgar Square a few days earlier and when the 20,000 demonstrators, organised in marches from all over London, converged on the Square, they fought with the mounted and foot police. The Riot Act was read and mounted armed troopers called in. There were a large number of injuries on both sides. Two demonstrators died of their injuries and 160 served prison sentences.

Field and Dickens

One of the people responsible for endearing Scotland Yard to the people was Charles Frederick Field. He had been with the police force since its inception and was a particularly good friend of the writer Charles Dickens. Dickens, in search for inspiration, accompanied Field many a time on his night rounds. There followed an essay titled *On Duty With Inspector Field* that appeared in the papers. It was flattering and portrayed the Met and its staff in a positive light. The writer also went on to model the character of Inspector Bucket of *Bleak House* on that of Field.

Sir Richard Mayne

According to many historians, Sir Richard Mayne, one of the first commissioners of the Met, was unhappy with the rules delegated to the new-formed police. Policemen were barred from making any investigations and any effort to discover offenders. The only recourse available in such a case was to try to catch the culprit red-handed. Mayne secretly started to train a few men in his department in the art of investigating. His wisdom became apparent when in 1840, the Whig politician Lord William Russell was murdered while asleep in his apartment. Mayne was directly involved in solving the case and took this opportunity to test the skills of the men he had been training undercover for ten years.

These new detectives accompanied Mayne to Lord Russell's house and started to collect evidence in order. They were successful. It was Lord Russell's own butler who had committed the crime and had kept both the money and the murder weapon in the house. Yet, despite their success in solving this high-level murder case, it was still not the right time for the secret detectives of Scotland Yard to openly make their presence felt.

Mayne's Hammer on Hot Iron

The opportunity Mayne was waiting for arrived two years later in 1842, when a man named John Francis attempted to assassinate Queen Victoria in her carriage on The Mall in London. The incident struck fear in the hearts of all parliamentarians and Mayne presented his case for the presence and need for a detective department within the Met. He consolidated his argument by saying that such a situation would not have occurred in the first place if the police had a little more power and investigative allowances. Consequently, after two months the Detective Department of Scotland Yard was established.

Idealised Met detectives

To begin with, there were eight detectives and their flair for investigating crimes made a lasting impression on the public's imagination. This was further substantiated by fictional crimewriters who set up the image of an intelligent detective in trench coat, top hat and a tobacco pipe, going about busting hardcore criminals. In Conan Doyle's Sherlock Holmes series, Holmes though a private detective, stood for the ideals that had become synonymous with the sleuths of this extraordinary London force.

The Bermondsey Horror

One of the most shocking crimes of Victorian England was the so-called "Bermondsey Horror". This gruesome crime, engineered by a woman, shook a society that considered the fair sex incapable of such evil. In August 1849, Scotland Yard successfully investigated the murder of Patrick O'Connor by husband and wife Frederick and Marie Manning. O'Connor, the lover of Mrs Manning, was brutally murdered for money and property by the couple, who then buried the body under the slabs of their kitchen. The body was discovered a few days later and the Met detectives made use of the latest technology to crack the case and arrest the culprits from two different locations. They were publicly hanged in November, a gruesome sight that led Charles Dickens to write a letter to the Times with a plea to discontinue such morbid displays that, unhappily, were enjoyed by the spectators.

Dick Tanner of the Yard

Railways, the child of industrialisation in England, had changed the geographical and economic face of the country. The possibility of being able to travel at speed had extended the seams of the metropolis of London, with many middle-class working people setting up house in the suburbs. One night in July 1864, the body of Thomas Briggs was found unconscious on the railway tracks near Hackney. He had sustained serious head injuries and died a day later. The search was sparked by two passengers who, late in the evening, found a bloody, but empty first class compartment.

Richard Tanner, 31 years old at the time, was one of the most promising Met detectives; he was immediately put on The Case of the Railway Murder. He discovered that a gold chain and top hat belonging to the businessman was missing and immediately sent out reward notices for people who could provide information. A silversmith and a taxi driver came forward with details regarding a German by the name Hans Muller, who had left for America in an unusual hurry. Tanner made use of the train and fast moving steamship to reach America, almost three weeks earlier than the prime suspect. Briggs's gold chain and top hat were found in the luggage of Muller upon his arrival in New York. It was evidence beyond doubt about Muller's guilt. More than fifty thousand people came to witness the public hanging of Muller in November 1864 and applaud the swiftness with which Tanner brought about justice in the case.

Making of the CID

Lieutenant Colonel Rowan died in 1852, after which Scotland Yard was overlooked single-handedly by Commissioner Mayne. By the 1870s, the police force had become an inseparable part of London's social, economic and political life. But it did not come as a surprise when three of its high-ranking detectives were convicted and sent to jail for two years on charges of corruption in a gambling case in 1877. The Home Ministry was shaken out of its complacency and forced to take stock.

After a thorough investigation, the detective department was abolished in 1878 and the Criminal Investigation Department set up. Instead of being answerable to the Commissioner of Police, this department headed by C.E. Howard Vincent, was directly answerable to the Home Ministry. There were 800 men who worked in this newly formed unit. With immediate effect, the CID invested its time and energy in keeping criminal records, an idea that was to emerge as one of the fundamental resources for tracking down criminals.

Move to Victoria Embankment

With the rising number of people working for the Met and the CID, the original Great Scotland Yard buildings became increasingly insufficient. A move to an Italian-inspired stone building in Victoria Embankment was planned in the latter half of the 1880s. It is an ironic coincidence that the huge building was made out of stone quarried by convicts. Despite the change in address, the name Scotland Yard, which had by now become a metonym for the Met, was to remain.

The Whitechapel Murders

While the move to the new location was being planned and executed, Scotland Yard met with one of its most daunting tasks to date. It was a rendezvous with perhaps one of the first serial killers... Jack the Ripper. It was in the autumn of 1888 that the country was shaken by the violent murders of five women in the Whitechapel area of the city. Scotland Yard used every conceivable resource and method then known, to try to hunt down the culprit, but was unsuccessful. The case required extreme ingenuity on the part of the investigators and led to the development of detecting techniques that are today still used in crimes scenes.

Whitechapel was one of the most impoverished areas of East End London, notoriously famous for immorality and crime. The Ripper chose all his victims from the area who shared very similar social profiles. The first incidence was when one among the 1500 prostitutes that walked the streets of Whitechapel was brutally murdered in the early hours of 7th August 1888. Martha Tabram's mutilated body was found in the George Yard Buildings. The mutilated bodies of other women were found in quick succession within a period of three months. The other victims were Mary Ann Nichols, Annie Chapman, Elizabeth Stride, Catherine Eddowes and Mary Jane Kelly. All of these women were prostitutes and with the exception of Kelly were middle aged. They were all murdered in a similar fashion in the dead of the night.

As observed in earlier murder cases, the culprit was always someone known to the victim. But the absence of any such links in these murders managed to completely befuddle the investigators. There was no precedent for serial killings that

A photograph of Albert Victor, Duke of Clarence and Avondale, elder son of Edward VII. Police suspected that Jack the Ripper may have been a well-educated man, and Albert Victor was a prime suspect, 1888.

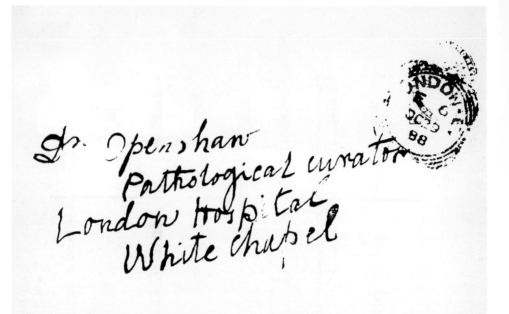

A sample of the handwriting that may have belonged to Jack the Ripper, and was taken from one of his letters to the police, 1888.

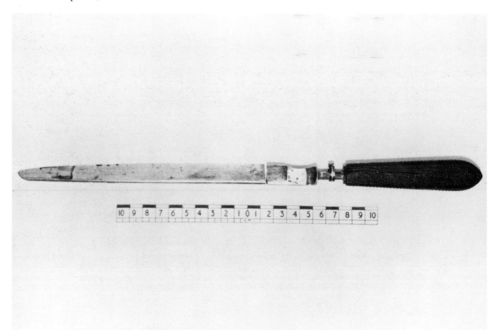

One of the knives used by Jack the Ripper in the Whitechapel killings in the East End of London, 1888.

A portrait of Sir William Gull, a well-known physician in the 19th century who is remembered for making a number of significant contributions to medicine during his lifetime. Since the 1970s, Gull has also been a suspect in the Jack the Ripper case, 1888.

A photograph of Robert James Lees, an English spirit medium who claimed to know the identity of 'Jack the Ripper' during the time of the Whitechapel murders, 1888.

WHITECHAPEL, 1888.

First Member of "Criminal Class." "FINE BODY O' MEN, THE PER-LEECE!"
Second Ditto. "UNCOMMON FINE!—IT'S LUCKY FOR HUS AS THERE'S SECH A BLOOMIN' FEW ON 'EM!!!"

"I have to observe that the Metropolitan Police have not large reserves doing nothing and ready to meet emergencies; but every man has his duty assigned to him, and I can only strengthen the Whitechapel district by drawing men from duty in other parts of the Metropolis."—*Sir Charles Warren's Statement.* "There is one Policeman to every seven hundred persons."—*Vide Recent Statistics.*

A satirical illustration commenting on the shortage of police officers around the time of the Whitechapel murders, 1888.

L. Forbes Winslow, an English Psychiatrist who claimed that he knew the identity of Jack the Ripper, and believed that if he was given a team of six Police Constables he could catch the murderer, 1888.

BLIND-MAN'S BUFF.

(As played by the Police.)

"TURN ROUND THREE TIMES,
AND CATCH WHOM YOU MAY!"

A satirical illustration depicting the game 'blind-man's buff', and commenting on the powerlessness of the police during the Whitechapel murders, 1888.

An illustration depicting self-appointed 'vigilantes' in the East End of London looking suspiciously at a dubious- looking passer-by, during the time of the Whitechapel murders, 1888.

could be referred to for insights, and Scotland Yard had to come up with strategies on its own.

The assistant commissioner of police commissions Police Sergeant Dr Thomas Bond looked for links between all these murders in an attempt to gain the slightest of clues. But the art of criminal science and investigation was in its infancy and there was only so much for the detectives to work with. Dr Bond created what is known as the criminal profile after closely studying each of the killings, the profiles of the victims, the manner in which they were killed, the days on which they were killed, and so on.

This was perhaps the first criminal profile ever made in the history of criminal investigations – something that has become standard procedure today. The profile included an insight into the characteristics of the killer, including the murderer's profession, area of residence, the use of the right, or left hand for the killings, the murder weapon and similarities between the victims. With the overactive media, the news of these murders spread like a forest fire and Scotland Yard was flooded with letters from hundreds of people.

It was at this time when a letter, allegedly sent by the killer, was received at headquarters. It was signed 'Jack the Ripper'. The police also received another letter that was titled 'From Hell', which was sent with a piece of human kidney. The killer in the letter claimed to have eaten a part of it. This piece of information was interesting in that it implied cannibalism was part of the killing. It was as if the killer was mocking the investigation.

In a desperate attempt to find a resolution to the horror, Charles Warren, the then police commissioner, instructed the investigators to make use of bloodhounds or sniffer dogs at crime sites to lead to the culprit. It was shortly after the experiment of this new method that the killer struck again. This time it was the unfortunate Mary Jane Kelly who was found mutilated. This was to be the first time the police would barricade the entrance to the crime scene in an effort to preserve every shred of evidence. She was the only Ripper victim who had been murdered indoors and the police took the first ever crime scene photographs in history.

Despite extensive investigations and thorough interrogations of people evenly faintly related to the victims, the Ripper murder cases were never solved. The investigators just ended up with a long list of possible suspects and no conclusive evidence against anyone. Then the terror of the Ripper that had struck at the heart of England, suddenly disappeared into thin air. Through failing to find the culprit and provide justice and dignity to the victims, this case proved to be an important milestone in the history of Scotland Yard. The methods and techniques used in the investigative process in this case marked the beginning of a new era of sophistication in such processes.

The following were some of the officers who played a part in investigating the mysterious murders: Inspector Frederick Abberline, Sir Robert Anderson, Inspector Walter Andrews, Superintendent Thomas Arnold, Detective Constable Walter Dew, Detective Sergeant George Godley, PC James Harvey, Inspector Joseph Helson, Chief Inspector John Littlechild, Sir Melville Macnaghten, James Monro, Chief Inspector Henry Moore, PC John Neil, Inspector Edmund Reid, Detective Constable Robert Sagar, Major Henry Smith, PC William Smith, Inspector John Spartling, Chief Inspector Donald Swanson, Sergeant William Thick, PC Ernest Thompson, Sir Charles Warren, PC Edward Watkins, Sergeant Stephen White and Chief Constable Adolphus Williamson.

Ponderings by Investigators

It was in the year 1892 that the case of Jack the Ripper or the Whitechapel murders was officially closed owing to the lack of any concrete leads and a long list of probable suspects. The horror of the case left an indelible mark on officials, and a few of them, during latter day interviews and writings, pondered on the identity of the Ripper.

The theories were so different that no conclusive fact could be discerned. Many believed that the Ripper was already dead or had been put in an asylum. Robert Anderson was the only officer who hinted to the complete knowledge of the murderer and hinted towards Kominski, a Polish Jew, who was a major suspect in the case. Even Swanson seemed to be inclined in that similar direction, but there were discrepancies in the theory. Macnaghten also introduced him as one of the primary suspects in some of his writings published at a much later date. The lack of resolution in the Whitechapel murders can in no way taint the efforts made by Scotland Yard to uncover the murderer. If anything, it pointed to the lack of scientific expertise available to investigators for solving such cases.

However, undeterred, Scotland Yard proved its mettle time and again, even while stepping into the 20th century with a changed political, social and economic environment.

Chapter 10
The Suspects

The Suspects

In addition to other unlikely candidates over the years, some researchers have suggested that Jack the Ripper may have actually been a female, dubbed 'Jill the Ripper'. The proposal is that she may have been a midwife, perhaps unable to bear children of her own, attacking other women – prostitutes – who could have children. Women would have been more willing to go off with other women, taking risks that they may not with a man. Additionally, it is possible that a midwife would have knowledge of the human anatomy, particular the female anatomy, which would explain the precision with which the bodies were mutilated.

With the gruesome and unique nature of his crimes, it would seem there would be a limited number of suspects that could be lined up as Jack the Ripper. However in the years since the killings, hundreds of names have come under the scrutiny of authors and investigators. Jack himself never came forward to brag of Scotland Yard's incompetence or to demonstrate Ripper-only knowledge of the brutal slaughters. Even in later years, only one record was uncovered that ever truly gave a clue about who could have been the Ripper. Means, motive and opportunity, of course, are critical to finding the correct suspect.

During the time of the murders, the police and newspapers received many tips and letters about the Whitechapel killer. The sheer amount of correspondence was overwhelming, and the police deemed the majority of the letters to be written by reporters themselves or created by sensationalists, particularly because of their failure to demonstrate exact knowledge of the crimes. Letters of particular note were those saying "Dear Boss", "Saucy Jacky" and "From Hell".

None provided information that led to any suspects and later they would be identified as publicity stunts and practical jokes. However, the "Dear Boss" letter was particularly alarming as it promised to cut the next victim's ears off and post them to the police. The "Saucy Jacky" postcard seemed to have unpublicised information concerning two of what were then most recent deaths – Stride and Eddowes. The "From Hell" letter came with a disturbing item: half a human kidney that was confirmed by a doctor who identified it as the left kidney such as was missing from Eddowes. However, the kidney's owner could not actually be identified and afterwards journalists would take responsibility for many of the letters.

No single identifying factor unites the suspects. They were from different economic and social classes, different professions, had varying marital statuses, various degrees of previous criminal activity, different countries of origin and even differing degrees of mental stability. Though a number of people believed they had seen the murderer, no two descriptions of him were the same. The only certainty was that they perceived him to be a man. A man of varying heights by the accounts. Some found him to be fair and others dark, he either wore the clothes of a poor man – dishevelled and downcast – or he was suave and wore the threads of wealth and power.

While no items of evidence were available to clearly identify the killer, police pursued and questioned many individuals and remained suspicious of eight in particular: Thomas Cutbush, Montague John Druitt, Seweryn Klosowski, Aaron Kosminski, Michael Ostrog, John Pizer, James Thomas Sadler and Francis Tumblety. Over the years, the most strongly held beliefs were for Cutbush and Kosminski, who were both later institutionalised, Druitt, who committed suicide, or Ostrog, who travelled extensively.

Seweryn Klosowski (1865–1903), also known as George Chapman, was a Polish immigrant who lived in Whitechapel during the murders. Inspector Frederick Abbeline suspected him, owing to his conviction for the murders of his three wives, all of whom were poisoned. Klosowski was found guilty of murder and hanged. It could be perceived that his prior crimes had been the murder of prostitutes. Many current researchers dismiss him as a potential suspect because of today's understanding of modus operandi, which suggests that serial killers operate in a specific way as part of their routine and mindset. While possible, it is unlikely that a killer of such violent tendencies, particularly in organ removal and mutilation, would be sufficiently content with the simple killing by poison.

John Pizer (1850–1897) was considered a vicious man, driven to violence and accused of a number of minor assaults on prostitutes. His prior assaults made him an easy suspect, however, he was not a willing suspect. Locals of Whitechapel referred to him as the "Leather Apron" and many suspected he truly was Jack the Ripper, even after the police dismissed him owing to his alibis concerning at least two of the Canonical murders. With no evidence, Pizer was cleared as a suspect. He went on to challenge publications accusing him of being the Ripper and from one was awarded compensation.

James Thomas Sadler was on the prime suspects' list owing to his violent tendencies and known company of prostitutes. He personally knew one woman who died and was even arrested in connection with her murder, however, police failed to find any true evidence against him and he was released. He was dismissed as a possible Ripper suspect because he was at sea during the Canonical murders. Later he was referred to as merely a drunk with a terrible temper.

Francis Tumblety (1833–1903) had a colourful background in both the United States and Canada. Although he was believed to have been connected to at least one patient's death during his time as an Indian herb doctor, and later arrested in connection with the 1865 assassination of Abraham Lincoln, Tumblety remained outside of prison. His connection to the crimes is believed to be impossible owing to conflicting accounts of his imprisonment.

In 1888, Tumblety was arrested for homosexuality in England and fled to France, later returning to the United States, where he was believed to have been detained during the time of at least one of the Canonical Five murders. While the arrest in England was not in association with the Whitechapel murders, it was widely reported as such in America, and later Chief Inspector John Littlechild would list him among possible suspects in his report.

Thomas Cutbush lived between 1865 and 1903. Accounts of him describe him as a delusional individual suffering from syphilis and prone to violent outbursts. On one occasion, he stabbed a woman and in another incident nearly hurt a family member. His behaviour, and choice of weapon, made it believable that he could have been the Ripper. In later years, writers would suggest that his institutionalisation in 1891 was the reason why the murders stopped. Some people believe that his particular condition did not lend itself to the murders, because he did not confess to them at any time during his life in the asylum.

Others still believe that he was both capable and had the opportunity to commit each of the violent crimes. Later, Sir Melville Macnaghten would completely dismiss him as a suspect. However, it was suggested that he did so not on the basis of evidence, but out of respect for Cutbush's uncle, a police officer, whose reputation could be harmed by his nephew being on the Ripper suspect list.

Scotland Yard's Assistant Chief Constable (1889–1890), Sir Melville Macnaghten, gathered up the records and pursued the case himself, writing, "The truth, however, will never be known." The documentation and research conducted by Macnaghten did not take place until after the primary investigations and the end of the killings. However, he identified the five victims most likely to have been killed and mutilated by the Ripper, calling them the Canonical Five. During these results, he dismissed the idea that Cutbush was the serial killer, and identified three other possibilities, based on the evidence and information he had gathered. This work was never investigated until its release in 1959, which is when much of the current research began.

Sir Melville Macnaghten identified three of the most likely suspects as Montague Druitt, Aaron Kosminski and Michael Ostrog. Their selection was based on evidence, circumstances, known behaviours and possibly owing to conversations with friends or relatives. While Macnaghten is believed to have dedicated a great deal of time to his research, it is noted that information submitted in this report was not wholly accurate. One example is in the age and profession of Druitt, and another was the fact that no single person identified Kosminksi as the killer, but rather stated that they could not submit evidence against a fellow Jew.

Montague Druitt (1857–88) was a primary suspect for a number of reasons, but possibly the most compelling evidence was that his suicide coincided with the end of the Ripper murders. Montague was also close to a relative who was a doctor and may have picked up some anatomical knowledge from him. Druitt, who suffered from possible mental illness, lived within walking distance of the East End. His family suspected him and in his suicide letter he stated he did not want to be a burden.

Another suspect was Aaron Kosminski (1865–1919), and this was possibly due as much to his Jewish heritage and hatred of women, as any actual circumstantial evidence. A Jewish connection was made owing to the number of Jewish immigrants in the area and the possible Ripper evidence found on a wall that read, "The Juwes are the men that Will not be Blamed for nothing." However, there was nothing that created a strong link between Kosminski and the crimes and though he did suffer from mental illness, his condition did not lend itself to him being a murderer. His failure to brag about the murders works against the theory, as he suffered from paranoia, which leads to a constant desire to share in perceived accomplishments through boasting. Another reason why Kosminski was listed as a suspect included his interest in "solo" activities and was based on perceived behaviours of people who engaged in self-pleasure.

The third primary suspect, according to Sir Melville Macnaghten, was Michael Ostrog (c.1833–1904), who was said to be a professional conman and a former surgeon in the Russian Navy. He was thought to have been present in London during some of the Canonical murders and was believed to have the appropriate skills. Macnaghten found him a strange individual who carried around a number of knives and surgical equipment for no apparent reason. Yet Ostrog did not display any motive for such murders, and over the years, evidence placed him in France at the time. No evidence of his death exists.

At the time, the newspaper industry was a growing phenomenon and the case was published all over the world – a situation that continues to this day. The investigation and study of the Ripper has since created Ripperologists and resulted in a great number of suspects being added to the lists. They include Thomas Niell Cream, Frederick Bailey Deeming, William Henry Bury, Robert Donston Stephenson and Carl Feigenbaum.

Joseph Barnett (1858–1927) became a suspect owing to the Mary Kelly murder, the final and most violent of the Ripper killings. Her body was mutilated almost beyond recognition and suspicion arose that the murder had not been done by Jack the Ripper, but another person trying to imitate him. Barnett had previously been in a relationship with Kelly and when he lost his job on a fishing boat, she returned to prostitution. This was believed to have been what led to the murders of the other prostitutes, and eventually her. However, after four hours of questioning, police released Barnett and did not include him in their list of suspects. Barnett was not the only suspect suspected of killing only Kelly, but eventually it became accepted that she was among the Canonical Five because of Macnaghten's report.

A connection between Prince Albert Victor Edward and a Freemason was probed leading to conspiracy theories. Some of them, particularly since 1959, have suggested that the Freemasons led the murders in defence and protection of the Royal family, to either address the issue of the Prince's promiscuity or to investigate and study the causes of infertility. Others have suggested that the Freemasons committed the murders and the graffiti was code, specifically that "Juwes" represented the three murderers responsible for the death of the master mason of Solomon's temple, Jubela, Jubelo, and Jubelum. Conspiracy links to the Freemasons include everything from elaborate explanations of how the murders actually map out demonic symbols, to hidden passageways that permitted the Mason killers to escape unseen. These claims are typically unsupported by any evidence and rarely have the support of researchers, however, they are fondly used in fictional accounts.

Royal physician William Gull was perceived as a candidate for the Ripper in an attempt to prevent the blackmail of the royal family. It is suggested that Prince Albert Victor Edward was promiscuous and that the removal of the women's organs, particularly the uterus, was to prevent anyone discovering that they were pregnant. Some evidence was believed to support this, including that his wife may not have known his whereabouts at the time of the murders and that other suspicious activities occurred around the doctor. In addition, there are tales of another doctor in the same area being responsible for the murders.

Many of the tales directly related to Gull are a direct result of unsubstantiated evidence developed in the 1900s. A number of circumstances relating to his possibly being Masonic and insane created a scary image of the physician. Some of this is a result of the stroke he suffered, which also meant he could not have been the murderer owing to the condition the stroke left him in. Newspaper articles in 1895 suggested Gull as a suspect, and mediums and psychics have also named him as the killer. Yet Gull was reportedly in a mental institution during the crimes and he was not a skilled surgeon, only a physician.

The Duke of Clarence and Avondale – Prince Albert Victor Edward (1864–1892) was promoted to suspect as part of the Gull theory, but there is little support and no evidence. Some authors, in the late 1900s, suggested the Prince was on a killing spree with his lover, his tutor James Stephen. While some conspiracy theorists have believed him to be at best a reason for the murders, few have accused him of being the Ripper. The Duke's activities were widely documented and the likelihood of any evidence becoming available to the contrary would be unlikely.

Sir John Williams was the physician to Princess Beatrice and joined the suspect list in 2005, owing to the claim that all the victims knew the doctor and were killed as part of his research into infertility as his wife was infertile. It remains unclear, however, why the research would have ended so abruptly, or why the final victim would have been so mutilated. However, it was believed that doctors conducted illegal research on patients and sometimes made mistakes. However, another author suggested that it was the doctor's wife herself killing the prostitutes, because they could have children and she could not. It is believed that she became obsessed with her infertility. None of these claims includes any verifiable or supportive evidence.

James Kenneth Stephen (1859–1892) was a tutor for Prince Albert Victor Edward and became a Ripper suspect in 1972, when an author claimed he could have been involved because of his sexual attraction to the Prince and his intense jealousy over the women the Prince visited. Stephen committed suicide following the Prince's death. It is believed that the tutor may have loved the Prince so much it became an obsession that drove him to madness. In 1978, another author claimed to have discovered evidence of the tutor and Prince having a love affair and committing the murders together as part of some shared event. The connection was supposedly based on written notes that documented the Prince under hypnosis, written by Gull. The documents supposedly suggested that he actually died of an overdose of morphine that was the direct result of the ruling household. However, no such files or documents have ever been uncovered.

Alexander Pedachenko (1857–1908) was in another conspiracy related theory to the murders. This suggests that Pedachenko was an agent of the Russian secret police, who sent him to London to commit crimes against the people. They said that, with accomplices, he set out to demonstrate the ineffectiveness of Scotland Yard and discredit it. It was believed that the goal was to create public unrest, but no evidence supported this theory or the claim that Rasputin had written this in a document. No other evidence of either the suspect or the accomplices exists in any written records.

James Kelly (1860–1929) did not become a Ripper suspect until 1987 when researchers discovered that he had violent tendencies, had killed his wife with a knife stab to the neck, and had escaped the asylum where he was imprisoned in 1888. Researchers and authors uncovered evidence that he was suffering from mental instability, which could have demonstrated the correct mindset to commit the violent crimes.

He was also unaccounted for during many of the killings, and on top of the Canonical Five murders, may have been responsible for more crimes. Later, researchers believed him to have been perpetrating Jack the Ripper crimes throughout the US – a cold-case detective claimed that evidence linked Kelly to cities over the years where prostitutes were brutally murdered. His insanity was fairly well documented through a journal that said he had a deadly hatred of prostitutes and had taken actions against them. However, much of the information is not validated by published evidence.

Walter Sickert (1860–1942), a painter, was suggested as a possible accomplice to Jack the Ripper, if not the Ripper himself. His painting of a Ripper room, shrouded in darkness and mystery, encouraged people to suggest this may have been the case. Some assert his paintings and sketches follow a violently misogynistic theme. He even spent time in an apartment believed to have once housed the murderer. While little exists to demonstrate his actual connection to the Ripper or his victims, he maintained a fascination with the crimes. As with claims of an illegitimate son, no actual evidence has been found linking Sickert to the case.

James Maybrick (1838–1889) was a late addition to the list, having become a part of the research in the 1990s with the discovery of his journal, the "Diary of Jack the Ripper". He was a cotton merchant who lived in London and travelled often on business. He was believed to have been an arsenic addict, having begun taking it for an illness many years before his death from arsenic poisoning. He married a woman nearly half his age, Florence Maybrick, and it was suggested that his motive for becoming Jack the Ripper was his wife's infidelity. She would later be accused and tried as his murderer owing to his death from arsenic poisoning. After release from prison, she lived out her years in poverty in America. Florence and James had two children, who were raised by Dr Charles Chinner Fuller following their mother's conviction.

Maybrick's addiction to arsenic may have caused paranoia and schizophrenia, which could have created the state of mind required to have committed murder on that scale. However, no evidence, outside of the journal, demonstrated that he would have had the medical knowledge to commit the crimes. Maybrick had multiple residences and kept a mistress in one, but there is no evidence that he was in London during the Canonical Five murders.

Michael Barrett received the diary from his then wife Ann, who was believed to be directly related to Florence Maybrick. The journal graphically describes the murders, including evidence that could not have been known to anyone other than the killer, including the location of a tin box and coins set up neatly beside one of the victims. The journal, demonstrates the mindset required to commit such heinous crimes, graphically describing everything that occurred with a sense of the insanity expected in such a situation.

The journal underwent testing to determine its authenticity, including if the ink was the same compared to other writings known to be from Maybrick. No publications can agree how the many test results concluded, other than to say that not all of the handwriting matches. However, in 1993, additional information of evidence became available by way of a pocket watch, believed to be Maybrick's.

The watch, shown to the world by Albert Johnson, is said to have the words, 'J. Maybrick,' 'I am Jack,' and the initials of the Canonical Five. On two separate occasions the watch was evaluated and Dr Stephen Turgoose and Dr Robert Wild were not able to identify anything that would suggest that it was a fake, and said creating such a fake would be difficult to impossible. To date, no one has taken credit for faking the watch although some researchers say that this does not qualify as evidence.

Later when the journal was professed a fake, Michael Barrett took credit for the gruesome writings, then gave credit to Ann. To date, no clear story has been discovered from the two. Many researchers believe the diary to be a complete hoax; however, others hold on to the evidence that it could not have been written in the past 90 years, adding credibility based on the match to some of the Maybrick records.

Over the years, different people have come to be accused of being Jack the Ripper. The Whitechapel murders were not clearly defined as the act of a single individual and many people became involved in the story. After the initial outcry died down there was relative silence until interest was rekindled in 1959 with the Macnaghten papers.

Newspaper sensationalism has driven much of the research, but after 1959, the renewed interest resulted in Ripperologists taking up the investigation. While little of the evidence was available to review, over time more and more documentation has become available. Everything from cold-case techniques through psychic interventions have been involved in their search for the Ripper's true identity. However, as the crimes continue to both fascinate and appal it appears that, decades on, the quest to identify the Ripper will continue. By no means is the case closed.

Chapter 11

The Hoax Ripper Correspondence

The Hoax
Ripper Correspondence

> 'I was not codding [sic] dear old Boss when I gave you the tip, you'll hear about Saucy Jacky's work tomorrow double event this time number one squealed a bit couldn't finish straight off. Had not got time to get ears off for police thanks for keeping last letter back till I got to work again. Jack the Ripper'.

A murder investigation often relies significantly on help from the public and the media to get results. However, notorious cases always attract a unique type of person, the hoaxer. Hoaxers thrive off the publicity and drama such investigations bring. An experienced hoaxer can waste millions of pounds in human resources and more importantly, for the victim and their families, precious time. The public are often horrified and bemused at such people who get a thrill from interfering with an investigation.

These guileless fraudsters enjoy the power they have over the authorities, who may be clutching at every piece of information available to crack the case. Indeed, an experienced and intelligent hoaxer can stall the whole process and change the whole direction of an investigation. That is until the murder investigation is complete, then the whole game changes. The fraudster's power quickly fades and the hunt is turned on them. Modern-day law takes a tough line on people who obstruct investigations and many a hoaxer has been brought to justice.

Contemporary society has the advantage of being in the digital age and most lines of enquiries can be simply traced by digital footprints left by logins and internet usage. However, even with the most incredible advances in modern technology, a trickster can still be a difficult character to capture. Just imagine how difficult the task of tracking down a potential hoaxer would have been in the Victorian era?

It is still unclear which of the Ripper letters were authentic, but what is certain is that with the sheer volume most were hoaxes. Nevertheless, there were some notable letters that captured the authorities' attention and invariably changed the course of the investigation. It is a sorry fact that it will never be known if any of these sick hoaxes took the attention away from the actual perpetrator of the hideous crimes in London's East End in 1888.

The shocking twist in the Ripper investigation was that some of the hoaxes were believed to have been instigated by newspaper journalists. One of the embellished stories involved the self-styled "Dear Boss" letter, dated 25th September 1888, in which a character calling himself "Jack the Ripper" claimed responsibility for the Whitechapel murders.

In the autumn of 1888, hundreds of hoax letters were received by Scotland Yard and newspapers. The fact that the Ripper would not have had the time to kill and also spend so long handwriting hundreds of letters is proof that some of the letters were a hoax. There are, however, a notable few that did receive attention from the police and were taken at face value, although even the letters that were of interest cannot 100 per cent be proven as genuine.

"Dear Boss"

At first this letter, which was received on 27 September 1888, was dismissed as a hoax. The letter was delivered to the Central News Agency, a news distribution service founded by two brothers, William Saunders and his brother-in-law, Edward Spencer. Even before 1888, the agency had a reputation for underhand practices and rumours abounded that not all its stories were factually correct, or sometimes even true. It was once publicly accused and humiliated by The Times, who maintained that the agency embellished stories in order to undercut their rivals, The Press Association and Reuters. In order to prove this, the Times published a comparison between telegrams that were given to the Central News Agency and the telegrams that they went on to distribute to the public. One such telegram was a report on a naval battle between China and Japan that had taken place in the Far East, The Battle of Weihaiwei.

The original report provided to the Central News Agency was two hundred words and gave just overview information that the battle had taken place. Yet the version distributed to newspapers contained detailed narrative of the battle. The Times declared that the Central News Agency had deliberately embellished the report to make it more sensational and therefore of more interest to the public. It insisted that as much as two thirds of the article was different from the original and therefore had been manufactured by the Central News Agency, a fact that the Agency belatedly admitted, though claiming their literary expansion to be in the public interest.

It is with this somewhat dubious reputation that when the Agency in September 1888 declared to have a letter from the Whitechapel Murderer, the authorities did not pay too much credence to their revelation.

The letter was addressed "Dear Boss," and was in blood red ink with good legible writing at a slight slant, although it did contain spelling and punctuation errors.

> Dear Boss,
>
> I keep on hearing the police have caught me but they wont fix me just yet. I have laughed when they look so clever and talk about being on the right track. That joke about Leather Apron gave me real fits. I am down on whores and I shant quit ripping them till I do get buckled. Grand work the last job was. I gave the lady no time to squeal. How can they catch me now. I love my work and want to start again. You will soon hear of me with my funny

little games. I saved some of the proper red stuff in a ginger beer bottle over the last job to write with but it went thick like glue and I cant use it. Red ink is fit enough I hope ha. ha. The next job I do I shall clip the ladys ears off and send to the police officers just for jolly wouldn't you. Keep this letter back till I do a bit more work, then give it out straight. My knife's so nice and sharp I want to get to work right away if I get a chance. Good Luck.

Yours truly

Jack the Ripper

Dont mind me giving the trade name

PS Wasn't good enough to post this before I got all the red ink off my hands curse it No luck yet. They say I'm a doctor now. ha ha'

Scotland Yard were forwarded this letter on 29th September and initially placed it with the hundreds of other letters already received. Perhaps mindful of whom it was sent to and knowing the agency's reputation, officers considered it a hoax. Three days after the Central News Agency received the letter and the day after Scotland Yard received it, the Ripper struck again. At 1am on Sunday, 30th September, the body of Elizabeth Stride was discovered in Dutfield's Yard in Whitechapel. Elizabeth had a clean clinical cut to her left neck which had severed the main artery, unleashing an immense amount of blood, yet no mutilations were on her body, leading to some doubts as to whether she was in fact a Ripper victim. Three quarters of an hour after Elizabeth's body was discovered another corpse was found, that of Catherine Eddowes in Mitre Square, within the City of London.

The sight that greeted the police on arrival would have been markedly different to the murder scene of Elizabeth. Catherine's murder was one of the most brutal to date attributed to the Ripper. She had her throat slit and a massive deep and jagged cut was made along her abdomen, which was then clearly forcibly ripped apart. Catherine's left kidney had been completely removed as well as the majority of her uterus. Her face had been disfigured with slashes and part of one ear had been cut off.

Although it was Victorian times and crime scene details cannot be as quickly circulated as in modern policing, it does beggar belief that the missing ear had not caused immediate alarm to the police.

The envelope was postmarked three days before the murder of Catherine Eddowes and The "Dear Boss" letter had the chilling words:

> The next job I do I shall clip the ladys ears off and send to the police officers just for jolly wouldn't you.

When the post mortem information filtered through to the head office at Scotland Yard, one of the policemen remembered the letter from the Central News Agency. Suddenly the "Dear Boss" letter was of significance and the police retrieved it from the pile of hoax letters for forensic investigation. Although it is known that some police considered the Ripper story to be created by the newspapers, nevertheless it was to the press that the Yard turned for help in their investigation.

The police launched a public appeal and published extracts of the handwriting in the newspapers, hoping that someone would come forward if they recognised the style of handwriting. Alas, this was not to be, and no intelligence came back from the public that had any merit for the investigation. This was, however, the first time that the words "Jack the Ripper" had been published in association with the murderer, hitherto known as the "Whitechapel Murderer", largely because the murders were carried out there. However, and perhaps also owing to the killer's express intent given by the phrase he wrote after his signature:

`Dont mind me giving the trade name`

This "trade name" caught on and because some newspapers had published the letter in full, people outside of London were acquainted with the serial killer. Nothing catches the imagination more than a catchy brand name and the letter indicated that he didn't like being called "Leather Apron" and was effectively asking that he be called Jack the Ripper. The word ripper is mentioned in the letter more than once and is referred to in the earlier phrase:

> I am down on whores and I shant quit ripping them
> till I do get buckled.

Was this just a phrase which gave the author a private laugh as it was a play on his own created brand name, or was it a more sinister reference to the act of forcibly ripping open the flesh his victims? Coupled with the sensational violence of the murders, the "Dear Boss" letter and the name Jack the Ripper caught the attention of the rest of the world, a remarkable feat considering the communication methods of Victorian London.

What is perhaps more remarkable is that the "Dear Boss" letter was lost from the police files shortly after the investigation in the early 1900s. Incredulously, no police investigation was instigated at the disappearance of critical primary evidence. Adding to the mystique of the Ripper. The original letter was anonymously returned to the London Metropolitan police in 1988.

"Saucy Jacky"

If hoax letters were proving a nuisance and diverting the police away from their investigations, then perhaps consideration should have been given to what parts of the "Dear Boss" letter were published. The brand name of Jack the Ripper and the detailed intent caused a sensation, but they also encouraged individuals who felt compelled to write a hoax letter. Scotland Yard and the newspapers were now inundated with letters and postcards, and owing to the "Dear Boss" letter, these could not be so readily dismissed. Police manpower was massively taken up on reading each and every one before its usefulness could be assessed.

On the 1st October, 1888, the day after the murders of Elizabeth Stride and Catherine Eddowes, a postcard was received at the head office of the Central News Agency. It was immediately handed to Scotland Yard. After comparing the letter with the postcard, Scotland Yard concluded that, whether a hoax or not, the handwriting was remarkably similar between the two.

> I was not codding dear old Boss when I gave you the tip, you'll hear about Saucy Jacky's work tomorrow double event this time number one squealed a bit couldn't finish straight off. Had not got time to get ears off for police thanks for keeping last letter back till I got to work again.
>
> Jack the Ripper

As the text shows, this postcard was again signed off with the "brand name" Jack the Ripper, although bizarrely he plays on the name Jack and refers to the Ripper as "Saucy Jacky" – an oddity that suggests sexual overtones to the killings.

Yet one can only imagine the surprise on the face of the police officer tasked with the examination of the "Saucy Jacky" postcard. It was able to report on the two murders before they had been widely exposed. Further evidence that the "Dear Boss" and the "Saucy Jacky" correspondence was penned by the same author comes from him referring to the earlier letter in the opening line with:

> I was not codding dear old Boss when I gave you the tip

The word "codding" jars with the generally accepted public perception that the Ripper was an educated gentleman with surgical skills. Here, a basic spelling mistake of "kidding" occurs, which if these letters were genuine, would bring into question whether the author was literate and had a good education, something a medical professional or "gentlemen" of the time would have definitely had.

One belief is that the information revealed in the postcard was not detailed enough and was the same that residents and local London news journalists would have already known. However, there is absolutely no doubt that both were written by the same person, although as to whether it was the elusive Jack, remains a debated subject to this day.

Unfortunately, modern-day experts can only examine a facsimile of the "Saucy Jacky" postcard held in the archives and reproduced at the time from the original. Incredibly, like the "Dear Boss"

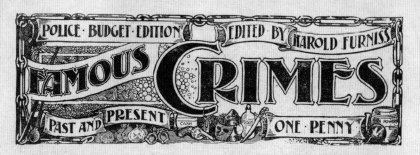

POLICE · BUDGET · EDITION   EDITED · BY · HAROLD FURNISS

FAMOUS CRIMES

PAST AND PRESENT   ONE · PENNY

HOW THE "RIPPER'S" VICTIMS WENT TO THEIR DEATH.

Vol. II.—No. 17.

An illustrastion that depicts how the Ripper's victims went to their death; the killer meets a street woman in a Whitechapel alley, and invites her to accompany him. 1888.

A Short Stout Man.

An illustration of 'a short stout man,' as possible eye-witnesses describe the man that could have been Jack the Ripper, 1888.

THE NEMESIS OF NEGLECT.

" THERE FLOATS A PHANTOM ON THE SLUM'S FOUL AIR,
     SHAPING, TO EYES WHICH HAVE THE GIFT OF SEEING,
INTO THE SPECTRE OF THAT LOATHLY LAIR.
          FACE IT—FOR VAIN IS FLEEING!
RED-HANDED, RUTHLESS, FURTIVE, UNERECT,
'TIS MURDEROUS CRIME—THE NEMESIS OF NEGLECT!"

An illustration of the Nemesis of Neglect, pinpointing crime as a result of the bad conditions in London, 1888.

'Sketches with the police at the East End'. A series of sketches during the Jack the Ripper murders showing suspects being arrested and on identity parades, 1888.

A photograph of Montague John Druitt, one of the suspects in the Ripper case; he was a well-known sportsman, scholar and barrister, born in 1857, and committed suicide in late 1888.

An illustration depicting Jack the Ripper commanding the respect of his confreres, 1901.

OUTCASTS SLEEPING IN SHEDS IN WHITECHAPEL.

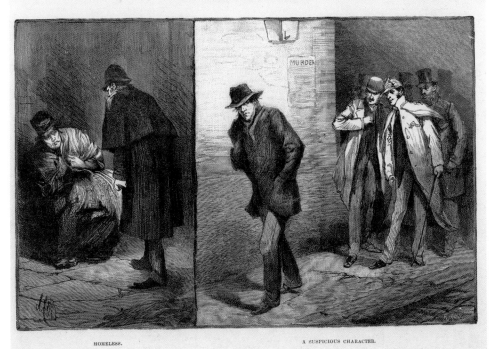

HOMELESS.   A SUSPICIOUS CHARACTER.

A group of illustrations showing Jack the Ripper with the vigilance committee in the East End of London, October 1888.

Film still from the 1959 film Jack the Ripper showing newspaper boys announcing another Jack the Ripper murder in London.

Still from 1959 film "Jack the Ripper" directed by Robert S Baker and Monty Berman.

letter, which went missing, the postcard disappeared from the case file some time in the early 20th century. Again, no investigation was launched at the time into why such a crucial piece of evidence could be lost when under lock and key in a secure vault at the police headquarters. Today, forensic experts are frustrated by the fact that the postcard is unavailable for further analysis, especially with the benefit of modern DNA and forensic science.

Whitechapel Vigilance Committee and the "From Hell" hoax

On 16th October 1888, hoax events took a disturbing turn when a cardboard box arrived at the offices of the Whitechapel Vigilance Committee. This organisation was formed on 10th September 1888 by a group of East End business owners who were concerned about what effect the Whitechapel murders would have on the community and, more importantly, local business. The first meeting of the committee took place in a pub, The Crown, where a man called George Lusk was voted in as chair.

The committee predominately was a pressure group that constantly lobbied the then Home Secretary, Henry Matthews, on the lack of progress in catching what was then a double murderer. They sought as much publicity on their campaign as possible, although it was the name George Lusk who was headlined. They printed appeal posters calling for help in identifying the murderer and highlighted their cause via the newspapers. Despite being publicly criticised by the group, Matthews held firm and flatly refused government help in putting up a reward for catching the Whitechapel murderer. This group's determination reflected how trade in the East End was affected as people steered clear of the area whilst the murderer was at large. Ironically, a century later visitors flock to the area to take in "Jack the Ripper" tours and visit the murder scenes.

Once Henry Matthews had refused any money from the government, the committee set about offering their own reward, even hiring their own private detectives to act separately from the Scotland Yard investigation. Yet the Whitechapel Vigilance Committee achieved little apart from furthering the public's fascination with the Ripper and bringing attention to the name of George Lusk.

As chairman of the committee, it was George's name that adorned the numerous posters and appeared in any newspaper interviews. Lusk was born in 1839. He was a working-class builder and decorator and not highly educated. He was a member of the Freemasons, although his stint within this secretive order was short-lived. After seven years he was expelled in 1890 for not being able to pay his membership fees. One can only wonder whether the fact that he couldn't afford the fees was owing to economic hardship as a result of the Whitechapel murders. This would explain the sheer desperation of the Vigilance Committee and why they were so critical of Scotland Yard and the government.

But it was the cardboard box addressed to Lusk in 1888 that perhaps caused the greatest shock to the committee. When George opened the package he was confronted with the stench of a decomposing human organ. It was half of a human kidney, and appeared to be dripping with blood red, although this was later proven to be an amateurish attempt at medical preservation using red wine. Inside the box was a letter now known as the "Letter from Hell", which read:

> From hell
>
> Mr Lusk
>
> Sor
>
> I send you half the Kidne I took from one women preserved it for you the other piece I fried and ate it was very nice. I may send you the bloody knif that took it out if you only wate a while longer
>
> signed
>
> Catch me when you can Mishter Lusk

At first glance one is drawn to the spelling and bad grammar. Aside from this, there were a few clues that led most Ripperologists to concur with the widely accepted view that the package was a clear, albeit sensational, hoax. The letter was sent some fifteen days after the "Dear Boss" and "Saucy Jacky" letters, but contained no similarities in language or phraseology. What if, however, those two letters were hoaxes and the "From Hell" package with the blood red kidney was actually from the killer? Neither of the "Dear Boss" nor "Saucy Jacky" letters contained any physical connection to a Ripper murder, although the general conclusion by those leading the murder investigation was that the kidney could have been appropriated from one of a number of sources, including local mortuaries.

Lusk acted admirably on receiving this package and immediately forwarded it to a medical specialist. The kidney was sent to the City of London Hospital where Dr Thomas Horrocks Openshaw carried out an examination. The Press Association circulated a report that he identified it as a left kidney, which was, in his medical view, similar to that removed from the recent murdered victim, Catherine Eddowes.

Dr Openshaw was quoted as saying that it was a "ginny" kidney and belonged to a female aged around forty-five years. A "ginny" kidney is termed as one that has been subjected to a sustained period of alcohol and is often found in alcoholics. He said the kidney had been removed within the past few weeks, a fact which gave it significant importance considering the time frame of the recent murders.

However, the published report that appeared in the Eastern Post and City Chronicle newspapers on the morning of 20th October is at odds with what was published on the same day by The Star and Daily Telegraph newspapers. These newspapers reported Dr Openshaw as stating that it was a human kidney and may have been from the left side.

Dr Openshaw forwarded the kidney to the City of London Police who then carried out their own medical examination. This examination is briefly mentioned in an internal police report that would not have been available to the public or newspapers. This report was submitted by Inspector James McWilliam of the City of London Police on 27th October, and the section regarding the "Lusk Kidney", as it is now commonly known, read:

> The kidney has been examined by Dr Gordon Brown who is of the opinion that it is human. Every effort is being made to trace the sender, but it is not desirable that publicity should be given to the doctor's opinion, or the steps that are being taken inconsequence. It might turn out after all to be the act of a Medical Student who would have no difficulty in obtaining the organ in...

The majority narrative of the report by Inspector McWilliam concerned the inquest into the murder of Catherine Eddowes as well as witness information. It is obvious that he felt he needed to mention the kidney within his report, yet the scant mention and dismissive tone suggests that the official opinion was that it was a hoax and not the kidney of the dead woman.

The Metropolitan police also produced a report on the orders of the government Home Secretary, probably owing to the sensational reports appearing in the press about the kidney likely being that of the murder victim. The report from Chief Inspector Swanson of the Metropolitan Police stated: Mr Lusk brought a parcel which had been addressed to him to Leman Street. He received it on 15th Oct and submitted it for examination eventually to Dr Openshaw curator of London Hospital Museum who pronounced it to be a human kidney. The kidney was at once handed over to the City Police, and the combined medical opinion they have taken upon it, is, that it is the kidney of a human adult; not charged with fluid, as would have been the case in a body handed over for purposes of dissection to an hospital, but rather as it would be in a case where it was taken from the body not so destined. In other words, similar kidneys could be obtained from any dead person upon whom a post mortem had been made from any cause by students or dissecting room porter.

As this report gives the official commentary on the sequence of invents including George Lusk and Dr Openshaw, it also gives a completely different view to that stated in the newspapers. It appears that yet again in the case of Jack the Ripper, the newspapers at the time had put their own spin on the event. Even today debates still rage about the "Lusk Kidney" and whether or not it belonged to Catherine Eddowes.

The "Dear Boss" and "Saucy Jacky" letters were grammatically hopeless but the "From Hell" note trounces them with atrocious spelling and even worse grammatical mistakes. Could this simply be explained as a hoax and dismissed as the work of an uneducated individual? Or, as a small minority believe, could the author be Jack the Ripper, and in fact one who was so highly educated that he possessed the literary excellence to be able to conceal his eloquence and deliberately make mistakes. To pay this notion some credence one only has to look at the letter and highlight those words that were misspelt:

> From hell
>
> Mr Lusk
>
> Sor
>
> I send you half the Kidne I took from one women prasarved it for you tother piece I fried and ate it was very nise. I may send you the bloody knif that took it out if you only wate a whil longer
>
> Signed
>
> Catch me when you can
>
> Mishter Lusk

Perhaps there could be a hidden code within this letter. Yet it is odd that a somewhat illiterate hoaxer could link together descriptive adjectives over what he did with the kidney:

...prasarved it for you...I fried and ate it was
very nise'

There were basic spelling errors over words that were common
in the day such as Mister and Sir. It seems at odds with someone
who clearly understood the silent k in knife and the silent h in
while, which an illiterate person would almost certainly have
misspelt. These facts, when accompanied with the use of advanced
vocabulary, such as the word "prasarved", lends weight to the
argument that this letter was indeed written by an educated man
attempting to portray himself as an uneducated individual –
an elaborate hoax similar perhaps to the letter itself.

Another link to the author of the letter being an educated
person masquerading as an illiterate, one, can perhaps be explored
by the unusual title, "From Hell". This seems an odd title and in
fact one wonders why such a letter would need a title at all. One
would assume the "From Hell" letter is the author's attempt at
suggesting that he is writing it from a dark place, a secret hell that
he is enduring alluding to an excuse for his deplorable crimes. The
word hell would also suggest that the author of this letter is, or has
been schooled, in religious beliefs of heaven and hell. In Victorian
London, a significant number of the population attended church
and held the principles of religion in high regard, regardless of
class or education.

Interestingly, some Ripperologists feel that this title carries more
significance than it suggests at face value and could be a secret clue

worthy of further investigation. Strangely, when one looks at the September 7th edition of the London Times in 1888, and in particular an advert for a book published one month before the "From Hell" letter, it chillingly has a similar title.

Letters From Hell 14th Thousand. From the Darfish. With an introduction by Dr. George Macdonald. In one vol., crown 8vo., 6s. 'Should be read by every thinking mind.'-Morning Advertiser.

The actual book, the advert is selling, is a Christian novel written by a Danish priest, Valdemar Adolph Thisted, which was originally written in Dutch and published in Copenhagen in 1866. It was translated into English in 1866 and went through several editions, including the one with a preface by Dr George Macdonald, published in 1884. The book covers disturbing sex, violence, lust and maternal issues all penned in the first person. The salacious details, whilst trying to convey an overtly religious and moral theme, are all perfect ingredients for a novel that Jack the Ripper would surely appreciate. If some Ripperologists are to be believed, this is more than a coincidence. It could also be imagined that the author of the "From Hell" letter would have a copy of the title on his bookcase. This also could lend credence to the belief that he was a person of some means and educated to a high enough standard to read translated Christian works – even those of a salacious nature.

But Ripperologists, and any experts interested in investigating the Ripper case are today denied any further research into the

"From Hell" letter as it too has disappeared. Time has also prevented another possible breakthrough. If the kidney had been available to modern-day scrutiny, then the question as to whether it belonged to Catherine Eddowes could have been answered by a DNA test comparing it with modern-day relatives. It is not to be.

Dr Openshaw Letter

On 29th October 1888 a letter was delivered to the London Hospital for Dr Thomas Horrocks Openshaw. The envelope containing the letter was clearly addressed and postmarked London E, OC29 88.

> Dr Openshaw, Pathological curator, London Hospital, Whitechapel.

Within the envelope was a handwritten letter penned in black ink with the following text:

> Old boss you was rite it was the left kidny i was goin to hoperate agin close to your ospitle just as i was going to dror mi nife along of er bloomin throte them cusses of coppers spoilt the game but i guess i wil be on the job soon and will send you another bit of innerds
>
> Jack the Ripper
>
> O have you seen the devle with his mikerscope and

```
scalpul a-lookin at a kidney with a slide
cocked up.
```

Before considering whether this letter was from Jack the Ripper or
if it can be dismissed as an obvious hoax, the question has to be
considered as to why this was sent to Dr Openshaw. This is the first
correspondence purporting to be from Jack the Ripper and certainly
the first received by Dr Openshaw. Dr Openshaw was widely
reported in the press as the doctor at London Hospital who received
the "Lusk Kidney" carried out the examination. His name,
profession and where he worked was published numerous times and
perhaps it is down to this that he became the chosen recipient of
this letter. If this is indeed true then this immediately casts suspicion
on whether the real Jack the Ripper would have written to
Openshaw, as he was not the police pathologist and was usurped by
the police in favour of their own pathologist, Dr Gordon Brown.

The envelope contains complicated words such as "Pathology"
and "Hospital", which are spelt correctly, yet this jars with the
author's bad spelling in the actual letter, including the hospital spelt
as "ospitle". Had the wording on the envelope been directly
copied, perhaps from a credit in the newspapers about Dr
Openshaw, but was the author of such limited intelligence that he,
or she, hadn't appreciated or understood the correct spelling of
hospital in the letter?

Even without the opinion of a handwriting expert it is not
difficult to immediately reach the conclusion that the author of the
Dr Openshaw letter is definitely not the same author who wrote

the "Dear Boss" or "Saucy Jacky" correspondence. This letter bears the hallmarks of the type of person the "Dear Boss" letter was trying to imitate. Unlike the "Dear Boss" letter, the Openshaw letter shows the lack of understanding of the silent k of knife and the classic signs of how someone with a basic education would spell uncommon words. The spellings of the following words display how someone lacking in literary skills would attempt to spell words akin to how they would be pronounced:

> Rite.. kidny... goin... hoperate... ospitle...
> dror... nife...throte... innerds... delve...
> mikerscope... scalpel...

The misspelling of "devil" as "delve", also suggests that the author of the Openshaw letter is someone who has not benefited from religious education either, which is at odds with the religious inference given by the "From Hell" correspondence.

Some experts believe that as the "Dr Openshaw" letter mentions the left kidney, then this marries with the "From Hell" letter and therefore was written by the same author. Although this view is not without merit, some believe that such was the vast amount of information published about the Dr Openshaw "post mortem" on the George Lusk kidney, that anyone could have the same knowledge as that given in this letter.

The "Dr Openshaw" letter remarkably disappeared from the London Metropolitan police archives in the early 20th century but came into the possession of Donald Rumelow, a former London

City Police officer, in the 1970s. Donald Rumelow is a renowned author and Ripperologist specialising in the crimes of Jack the Ripper. He donated the Openshaw letter to the Public Records Office, who in 2001 made the document available to the general public.

However, the discovery and public publishing of the Openshaw letter has allowed modern scrutiny to take place, with results that are both fascinating and intriguing. American literary crime author Patricia Cornwell published her own findings in a book, "Portrait of a Killer – Jack the Ripper: Case closed" in 2002. The fact that Cornwell entitled it "Case closed" caused such a controversy that she took out full page advertisements in two British newspapers with her own letter refuting that she was "obsessed" with Jack the Ripper. However, it is a widely known fact that Cornwell had spent reportedly as much as £3.3 million on her own investigation into the Ripper murders.

If one researches Wikipedia, then it appears that, under pressure from Ripperologists, Patricia Cornwell took out these full page advertisements to "refute" and "clarify" that the case was "far from closed".

Beyond the grave, Jack the Ripper is still causing trouble.

Chapter 12

Catch Me If You Can

Catch Me If You Can

> *Scotland Yard had a long list of suspects, and confronted over 200 people in their search for Jack the Ripper. There were no reliable witnesses, but plenty of theories. Who was the real culprit? Did he or she even exist? Could it be possible that Scotland Yard were covering up one of the greatest conspiracies of all time?*

The case of the Whitechapel Murders is a terrible landmark in the history of crime. Out of it emerged the dark figure of Jack the Ripper, probably the world's first serial killer, who despite a massive outcry, was never captured. Since the desperate days of the late 1880s, there has been no closure. Although there have been countless theories and suspects, the true identity of murderous Jack has never been verified.

Dickens and the Origin of the Myth

Jack the Ripper had a significant influence on the minds of the Victorians and he went on to become a mythological figure.

The East End backdrop to the Ripper's crimes was tellingly described by Charles Dickens, who was lauded for the realism of his novels. In his early years as a writer, one finds cheerfulness in the descriptions of the streets overflowing with people, shouting vendors, a city full of opportunities where even poverty was not morbid or hopeless. It was the romanticism of London that was close to Dickens' heart.

It is not surprising that with age and maturity, Dickens paints a darker side to the East End with the cruelty and violence and in Oliver Twist features the prostitutes Betsy and Nancy. Dickens' works are strongly rooted in real places and real people. He was good friends with Charles Frederick Fields, an officer at Scotland Yard and would often join him on his nightly rounds of the city. What he saw was not just poverty and starvation, but an endless despair. He exposed much of this ugliness before a beast called Jack turned it into a bigger nightmare.

The Making of the Suspects

In pursuit of the Ripper Scotland Yard officers confronted over 2,000 people and conducted investigations on more than 300 before finally detaining 80 suspects. They had come up with new methods of investigating, such as taking pictures of the victims and the crime scenes, making sketches, cordoning off the crime scene, and making suspect profiles. However, it was all in vain. None of the suspects were convicted owing to lack of strong evidence.

Owing to the interest an unsolved case always arouses, the list of suspects has kept growing. There are books, articles, and theses, published even now, which claim so-and-so to be the murderer, according to their theories and their deductions. At the time, there was massive speculation, with the police initially thinking that it was the work of local gangs trying to terrorise people. But this theory did not really find any support because none of the gang members were brought forward, despite the attention the case was receiving.

Then the idea of a single man being responsible originated and the police started to think of the case as the work of a serial killer. Further theories put advanced questions about whether the killer had a medical background because of the evisceration of the murdered women. Many claimed that the mutilation was not done with any finesse and the killer was more likely to be a butcher or slaughterman. The officials were quite convinced that the killer was from the Whitechapel area, owing to the familiarity and ease with which the crimes were committed. Based on these speculations and the authority of opinion of some of the officers involved in the investigation, there were five major suspects seriously considered as being Jack the Ripper.

Montague John Druitt

Montague Druitt was a barrister in London who also worked as a schoolmaster in Blackheath. He was considered to be the prime suspect, by Melville Macnaghten, an officer in Scotland Yard at the time of the murders. Druitt's body was found in the Thames at Chiswick, on 31st December 1888, having been reported missing shortly after the murder of the Ripper's fifth Canonical Victim, Mary Jane Kelly, in Miller's Court. There was a history of insanity in his family and Druitt himself confesses to going mad in a letter addressed to his brother.

One of the reasons he was a suspect is that the murders stopped after his disappearance. For many years after the murders, he was widely believed to be the culprit, but this line of argument is only circumstantial. Macnaghten got a lot of the facts regarding the man wrong.

Michael Ostrog

Michael Ostrog was a conman, often in trouble for robbery or petty crimes. He served several prison sentences and later showed signs of going insane. Macnaghten, while claiming Ostrog as a suspect, got many facts wrong about him and called him a Russian doctor with homicidal tendencies. He also said that Ostrog's whereabouts at the time of the murders were unclear, with no substantial alibis. Ostrog was put away in a mental asylum, but records show that he did not show any homicidal tendencies. He was never known to have attacked women.

Aaron Kosminski

Aaron Kosminski for a long time was considered as the most probable suspect in the Whitechapel murders by Macnaghten, and two other high-ranking officers at Scotland Yard, Anderson and Swanson. As recorded by Macnaghten, Kosminski was a Polish Jew, a misogynist, who was sent to an asylum because of his insanity. Anderson claimed that the single witness to one murder had positively identified Kosminski, but he had refused to testify as he was of the same faith. Though there were no names taken, it is almost positively certain that he was referring to Kosminski. Confusion started with reports from the asylum that claimed that Kosminski was not given to violent outbursts and did not show any homicidal tendencies.

George Chapman,
aka Seweryn Klosowski

George Chapman was a junior surgeon from Poland. He arrived in London in the late 1880s, just around the time when the murders in Whitechapel began to happen. He worked as a barber in the Whitechapel area and is supposed to have been a resident of the George Yard Buildings where the murder of Martha Tabram had taken place. He married three times and murdered all three of his wives with poison, these facts coming to light only in the 1890s.

It was in retrospect that he was considered a suspect for the Whitechapel murders. The lawyer, through his opening statement with details about Chapman's whereabouts and medical background during the trial, even convinced Abberline, an officer involved in the investigation of the 1888 murders, about his culpability. Experts later disqualified Chapman's status as a suspect, because if he was a man given to such a violent and brutal modus operandi, why would he kill his wives by giving them poison? Such behaviour, though not impossible, is highly unlikely in a serial killer.

Thomas Cutbush

A series of articles that appeared in The Sun in 1894, discussed at length the Whitechapel murders and without naming Cutbush, made him a prime suspect. It is to refute these claims that Macnaghten wrote a memorandum with his own theory about the real and possible suspects. Cutbush showed signs of insanity and was sent to an asylum. The reports claim him to be violent and have the tendency to hurt others. But owing to the authority of Macnaghten's claims, not much attention has been given to the exploration of Cutbush as the Ripper.

Freemason Conspiracy

One of the most sensational theories about the Whitechapel murders was the 'Freemasonry Conspiracy', as talked about in the book titled 'Jack the Ripper: The Final Solution', which was released in 1976. Written by Stephen Knight, the book supposedly exposes the Royal and British government's hand in the Whitechapel murders. Though widely discredited by authoritative Ripperlogists like Donald Rumelow, the theory has gained much acceptance in popular culture. That the government and Monarchy can stoop to such low levels in maintaining the status quo appears to seem credible to people today.

BBC's Jack the Ripper

The story that led to the book started in 1973 with the BBC's production of a television programme about Jack the Ripper, owing to a fresh surge of interest in the murders. This programme was an eclectic combination of fictional figures and real facts and aimed to solve the mystery once and for all. Since it was based on real documents, thorough research was conducted to unearth all information regarding the murders.

This led them to Scotland Yard, where a detective pointed them to Joseph Sickert – which is when the supposed conspiracy begins to take shape. Joseph Sickert was the son of Walter Sickert, an artist who was in the East End in 1888. Joseph briefly outlined a tale in which Prince Albert Victor, popularly known as 'Eddy', had formed a relationship with a common working–class Catholic girl called Alice Mary Crook. They had a daughter who was called Alice Margaret. When Queen Victoria came to know about the situation she was furious. Crook was not only a poor girl but, more importantly, a Catholic.

According to the story, this information had the potential to topple both the Protestant monarchy and the government as since the beginning of the century the people were on the verge of revolution. The Queen called in the support of the Prime Minister, Lord Salisbury, to take action. There was a surprise raid on the Cleveland Apartment where the couple was residing and

Eddy and Crook were separated from each other and taken away. This is where Sir William Gull, the Queen's personal physician came into the picture. Through his influence, the young mother was sent to a facility where she was the subject of wild experiments. She slowly went insane and died at one of the asylums in the early years of the 20th century.

This seems to lead nowhere at all to the murders that happened in Whitechapel, but there is a twist in the tale. Mary Jane Kelly, the Ripper's last victim, was discovered by Walter Sickert in one of the numerous poor houses that existed in London in those days. She was brought into Sickert's house to take care of Eddy and Crook's child, Alice Margaret. She was present in the house when the raid happened and was given charge of the young girl. Kelly, being very scared, put Alice Margaret under the care of nuns, and returned to East End London, only to fall into extreme poverty, alcohol addiction and prostitution. This is when she met Mary Ann Nichols, Elizabeth Stride and Annie Chapman. She became good friends with these women and shared her bizarre tale with them. These women saw a window of opportunity and started to pressurise Kelly to blackmail the government. But despite the depravity they were living in, they could not imagine the equal depravity of the Monarchy and the government in trying to save themselves from scandal.

Through a network of spies, Lord Salisbury soon came to know about the womens' plan, and along with Lord Gull, decided to take care of the matter. John Netley was the coachman who used to take Eddy to the apartment in the East End for his rendezvous with Sickert and Crook. Lord Gull, with his help, killed all these women one after the other and created the myth of Jack the Ripper who has been thought of as the killer ever since. Meanwhile, the story went, the Monarchy and the government have both got away scot-free and managed to maintain their rule.

According to Joseph Sickert, even Commissioner Anderson was involved in the cover-up of the crimes, saying that the murder of Eddowes was a mistake. They first thought of her as Kelly, but only later found out the truth. Maybe that is the reason that the vengeance is most visible in her murder. The body was mutilated to an extent of no recognition, and left behind a sight that would turn the dead in their graves.

When the researchers at the BBC ventured into further unearthing of information, they discovered that a woman by the name Alice Mary Crook did live in Cleveland Street in those times, and also had a daughter out of wedlock around the same time frame that Sickert was claiming it happened. Convinced of its authenticity, the BBC decided to include it in their representation of the case, where Joseph himself appeared in the last episode to corroborate the entire story. It is in this retelling of the story that the involvement of the Freemasonry conspiracy theory was first mentioned.

Stephen Knight and the Book

Stephen Knight, a young author in the 1970s, requested a series of interviews with Sickert, who agreed to it after some hesitation, as he did not want a lot of attention drawn to him. During the interviews, the basic plot started taking the shape of a full-fledged conspiracy in the mind of Knight. He had a disagreement with Sickert, who did not want to do the book and had only agreed to the publication of an article or two. Knight went ahead with his research, which implicated the Royalty of England in a conspiracy with the Freemasons. The story was the same as was told in the BBC documentary, but instead of Commissioner Anderson, it was Walter Sickert who was the third party to complete the murderous triangle with Gull and Netley. Thus originated the book, which was an instant sensation.

Most historians, theorists, and Ripperologists do not see any merit in the work, and discard it by citing far-fetched connections made by the author. Never officially accepted, the book did take over the imagination of other artists who adapted the story in their own works. Some of the noted works that followed on the footsteps of this grand conspiracy as re-told by Knight includes the film 'Murder by Decree', by Bob Clark, released in 1978, and the graphic novel 'From Hell', written by Alan Moore and Eddie Campbell. This novel was later adapted to a movie by the same title.

Stephen Knight begins his book by saying that 'Jack the Ripper is a misnomer', further venturing to explain how people think of the Ripper as this devilish man given to the stalking and killing of prostitutes. For him the horror is his supposition that it was in fact not just one, but two people who were the killers, along with the help of a third. The half-truths and blatant lies that had till then been suppressed was, he said, one of the most controversial actions taken by the British government.

For some readers the ideas have merit and do not seem improbable. Victorian England is viewed as then on the verge of a revolution that would have the power to topple the Monarchy. London was overflowing with people, a lot of them immigrants, and with the disillusionment of the working classes there was the growing belief in socialism. At best it was a life of complete hypocrisy and decadent indulgences. According to Knight, the fact that documents pertaining to the case were not revealed to the public was nothing but an attempt to keep the truth hidden and an orchestrated attempt by the government to bury the truth about Eddy and his stories.

According to the author, Lord Gull was one of the most prominent Freemasons, a secret society that powered the government and the Monarchy. The audacity and fearlessness with which the murders were committed are the hallmarks of the actions performed in a ritualistic way by Freemasons. In the book, Knight says that:

If Masonic supremacy appears in jeopardy, it is reestablished by a show of strength, by crimes of violence, perpetrated to demonstrate the continuing power of Freemasons for the benefit of Brothers abroad...

The murders of the women seems to have a standard approach, very much like a ritual, and is similar to the hell that was promised to the traitors of the Freemason society when they took their oaths – mutilation being one of the methods. It is through the creation of the myth of Jack the Ripper that the power structure is maintained. People react to the incidents with interest, fear, and grudging admiration, and there is an immediate shift of concern from the inefficiency of the government, to dealing with a new threat that is more immediate.

All this works well at the theoretical level and, in some way, endorses the idea of much-believed theories about the generation of myth and the way the powerful use it to serve their own ends. A lot of thinkers completely disregard this theory told by Knight, but what a reader may note is that people who have spoken out about the Freemasons have died in mysterious circumstances, including Mozart, author William Morgan, director Stanley Kubrick, and of course, Stephen Knight.

Francis Tumblety and the American Connection

There has been a renewed interest in the culpability of Francis Tumblety as the killer of prostitutes in Whitechapel in 1888. Born in an Irish family, he was a self-proclaimed doctor who offered organic treatments and was routinely thought of as a quack. He travelled greatly between the USA, Canada and England, and was supposed to be present in Whitechapel at the time of the murders. He was a known misogynist who was proud of his attitude towards women. His hatred for women, according to a lot of people, stemmed from his bad marriage with a prostitute. Always mired in some controversy wherever he was, he also dabbled in pornography.

Colonel Dunham was a guest at the dinner party organized by Tumblety that consisted only of men. He later testified about the proof of Tumblety's hatred for women by recounting how during the party, he had boastfully shown off his huge collection of women's reproductive parts preserved in jars that according to him, came from all classes of women.

Tumblety was considered a suspect by officers investigating the murders at the time. His name figures in some of the documents pertaining to the case. He was a resident on Batty Street, which is close to the area in which the murders took place. Tumblety's landlord reportedly called the police after the discovery of a blood-soaked shirt in his quarters. There is also evidence of a handwriting analysis that suggests the similarity of his style with one of the infamous letters received by the press and the police.

In the early years of 1890s, Tumblety became ill and was admitted into St Louis Hospital. In the inventory of the things he possessed was the presence of two pieces of very cheap imitation jewellery. This was odd, as the rest of his possessions mainly consisted of genuine gems. Annie Chapman, one of the victims of the Ripper, was supposed to have had two imitation rings that were not recovered from her murdered body.

Jack Does Not Exist!

In a theory propounded by Trevor Marriott, who served as a detective with the Bedfordshire Police, and has extensively studied the documents pertaining to the case, Jack the Ripper is only an urban legend. Marriott says that there were only five murders that were attributed to the serial killer when in actuality there were in total around 17 cases in which women were murdered in a similar manner, including those that took place in Germany and the USA. He says that the information about the case has been progressively distorted, and has, in the process, completely obscured the truth. According to him, Jack the

Ripper is just a persona, perpetrated and promoted by journalism, and Thomas Bulling to be specific. Bulling was a journalist with the Central News Agency based in London, and handled the crime beat at the newspaper. It was he who sent those letters to the press and the police and coined the term Jack the Ripper.

Catch Me If You Can

The cases of the Whitechapel Murders and Jack the Ripper are now buried in an endless labyrinth of speculations, theories and conspiracies.

This part of the East End story may have started with Dickens, who in his works mythicised London of the 19th century, but it turned a brutal corner with the Ripper, an inseparable part of the city's identity, coming out of its ugly underbelly. It was not difficult for people to accept the existence of such a monster given the atmosphere of fear and decay that loomed over the East End.

The case is clearly not over. It began with the terrible events that unfolded on the cold, dark autumn nights of 1888 and still goes on in the 21st century with more comment, more explanations and much fantasy. There are clearly still vast areas to be traversed in the case of Jack the Ripper.

The task of unearthing the real facts about the Ripper may seem impossible as there is so much conflicting information out there... and many people are still adding to the noise. But there is hope that someday, sometime, there will be closure on this mixture of truth and myth and the mocking call of 'catch me if you can' will be silenced.

Picture Credits

i(t) Mary Evans Picture Library, i(b) PVDE/Epic/Mary Evans; ii(t) Mary Evans Picture Library, ii(b) PVDE/Epic/Mary Evans; iii(t) Mary Evans Picture Library/David Lewis Hodgson, iii(b) Mary Evans Picture Library; iv PVDE/Epic/Mary Evans; v(t) Mary Evans Picture Library, v(b) Mary Evans Picture Library/ David Lewis Hodgson; vi Mary Evans Picture Library/DAVID LEWIS HODGSON; vii(t) Mary Evans Picture Library/DAVID LEWIS HODGSON, vii(b) Mary Evans Picture Library; viii(t) Mary Evans Picture Library, viii(b) Mary Evans Picture Library/DAVID LEWIS HODGSON; ix(t) Mary Evans Picture Library/DAVID LEWIS HODGSON, ix(b) INTERFOTO / Sammlung Rauch / Mary Evans; x(t) INTERFOTO / Sammlung Rauch / Mary Evans, x(b) Mary Evans Picture Library/DAVID LEWIS HODGSON; xi(t) Mary Evans Picture Library, xi(b) Mary Evans Picture Library; xii Mary Evans / Peter Higginbotham Collection; xiii(l) Tal/Epic/Mary Evans, xiii(r) Mary Evans Picture Library; xiv Mary Evans/Epic/PVDE; xv(t) Illustrated London News Ltd/Mary Evans, xv(b) Mary Evans Picture Library; xvi Mary Evans Picture Library; xvii Mary Evans Picture Library; xviii(t) Mary Evans Picture Library/DAVID LEWIS HODGSON, xviii(b) Mary Evans Picture Library/DONALD RUMBELOW; xix Illustrated London News Ltd/Mary Evans; xx Mary Evans Picture Library; xxi Mary Evans Picture Library; xxii Photo Researchers / Mary Evans Picture Library; xxiii Mary Evans Picture Library; xxiv Illustrated London News Ltd/Mary Evans; xxv Mary Evans Picture Library; xxvi Mary Evans Picture Library; xxvii Mary Evans Picture Library; xxviii Illustrated London News Ltd/Mary Evans; xxix Mary Evans Picture Library/DAVID LEWIS HODGSON; xxx Mary Evans Picture Library; xxxi Mary Evans / The National Archives, London. England; xxxii(t) Mary Evans/Epic/Tallandier, xxxii(b) Mary Evans Picture Library/Interfoto Agentur

Cover Credits

Silhouette of man in hat left: Everett Collection/Rex Features
Woman tl: pd.
Woman tr: The National Archives UK
Map: public domain